EARTH ELEGY

EARTH
ELEGY

NEW AND SELECTED POEMS

MARGARET GIBSON

LOUISIANA STATE UNIVERSITY PRESS

BATON ROUGE AND LONDON

1997

06   05   04   03   02   01   00   99   98   97   5   4   3   2   1

Designer: Melanie O'Quinn Samaha
Typeface: Bembo
Typesetter: Impressions Book and Journal Services, Inc.
Printer and binder: Thomson Shore, Inc.

LIBRARY OF CONGRESS CATALOGING-IN-PUBLICATION DATA
Gibson, Margaret.
    Earth elegy : new and selected poems / Margaret Gibson.
        p.   cm.
    ISBN 0-8071-2145-2 (cloth : alk. paper). — ISBN 0-8071-2146-0
    (alk. paper)
    I. Title.
    PS3557.I1916E28   1997   96-51458
811'.54—dc21   CIP

This volume includes poems from other volumes published by Louisiana State
University Press and copyrighted in the name of the author: *Signs,* copyright
© 1975, 1976, 1978, 1979; *Long Walks in the Afternoon,* copyright © 1978, 1979,
1980, 1981, 1982; *Memories of the Future: The Daybooks of Tina Modotti,* copyright
© 1983, 1984, 1985, 1986; *Out in the Open,* copyright © 1985, 1986, 1987,
1988, 1989; and *The Vigil: A Poem in Four Voices,* copyright © 1991, 1992, 1993.
The author offers grateful acknowledgment to the editors of periodicals in
which poems in this collection originally appeared, sometimes in slightly differ-
ent form: *Black Box, Clockwatch Review, Crab Orchard Review, Crazy Horse, Em-
bers, Friends Journal, Graham House Review, Iowa Review, A Letter Among Friends,
Michigan Quarterly Review, Mid-American Review, Minnesota Review, Missouri Re-
view, New England Review/Bread Loaf Quarterly, New Virginia Review, New York
Times, Northeast Magazine, Parnassus, Poet Lore, Poetry, Poetry Northwest, Potlatxch,
Prairie Schooner, Seneca Review, Sewanee Theological Review, Shenandoah, Southern
Review, Spoon River Poetry Review, Tendril,* and *Texas Review.* "At the Ravine," "In
Here" (appearing as "Mother/Daughter"), "A Ripple of Deer, a Metamorphosis
of Bear, a Metaphor of Mountains," and "Sycamores" were first published by the
Georgia Review, and "Clarity" and "So Entirely Vivid" by the *Gettysburg Review.*
"In January, One Morning . . ." appeared originally in *The Unicorn and the Gar-
den,* edited by Betty Parry (Word Works, 1978), and "Sarah" in *Elvis in Oz: New
Stories and Poems from the Hollins Creative Writing Program,* edited by Mary
Campbell Flinn and George Garrett (University Press of Virginia, 1992).

The paper in this book meets the guidelines for permanence and durability of
the Committee on Production Guidelines for Book Longevity of the Council
on Library Resources. ∞

for David

I would like to thank those who have, over the years, given their guidance and counsel and friendship: in particular, Hobart and Jean Mitchell and Jacqueline Janes; more recently, Peter Matthiessen. Words of Eihei Dogen come to mind:

> This old plum tree is boundless. All at once its blossoms
> open and of itself the fruit is born. It forms spring; it forms
> winter. It arouses wind and wild rain. It is the head of a
> patch-robed monk; it is the eyeball of an ancient buddha. It
> becomes grass and trees; it becomes pure fragrance. Its
> whirling, miraculous transformation has no limit. . . . Blos-
> soming is the old plum tree's offering.

CONTENTS

EARTH ELEGY
NEW POEMS

Stubborn   3

Earth Elegy   4

Harvest Elegy   6

Solace   8

Grief   10

Riven   11

Elegy to a Sculptor   12

Prayer Ascending, Prayer Descending   19

In the Retreat House of the Virgin Guadalupe   21

At the Ravine   25

Blessing   27

Chayote   29

In the Sweet Grass Hills   31

Indian Graves   34

Core   36

Sycamores   38

Crossing the Ohio at Sistersville   40

Clarity   41

So Entirely Vivid   43

To Say Nothing of God   45

Resolutions   51

Home Ground   53

THE VIGIL
1993

Kate   57

Jennie 59

Sarah 60

Lila's Dream 76

OUT IN THE OPEN
1989

A Ripple of Deer, a Metamorphosis of Bear,
    a Metaphor of Mountains 81

Green Pepper 82

Garlic 83

In the Field 85

Doing Nothing 87

In the Desert 88

Keeping Still 93

In Here 94

Out in the Open 96

In the Woods 99

Cactus Blooms 101

Beginner's Mind 102

Making Salad 104

Stalking the Light 105

In the Mountains 109

Rings of Fire 111

MEMORIES OF THE FUTURE
1986

Memories of the Future 117

Doctrines of Glass and Wood 119

Fire Doesn't Die 121

Doors, Opening As They Do 123

Fast Light 126

Darkroom Nights 129

In the Market 131

Vocation 133

Día de los Muertos   135

What Love Is   138

María   139

From a Single Center . . .   141

Home   144

LONG WALKS IN THE AFTERNOON
1982

Long Walks in the Afternoon   149

The Inheritance   150

The Onion   153

Affirmations   154

Ice Storm   156

To Speak of Chile   157

Burning the Root   158

Unwritten History   159

Radiation   161

October Elegy   163

Country Woman Elegy   165

Unborn Child Elegy   166

Glass Elegy   168

Gemini Elegy   170

Onion Elegy   171

Fire Elegy   173

SIGNS
1979

A Grammar of the Soul   177

Remembering What I Want   179

The Garden   180

A Simple Elegy   187

Signs: A Progress of the Soul   192

In January, One Morning . . .   200

Voices. Voices. Listen, my heart, as only
saints have listened: until the gigantic call lifted them
off the ground; yet they kept on, impossibly,
kneeling and didn't notice at all:
so complete was their listening. Not that you could endure
God's voice—far from it. But listen to the voice of the wind
and the ceaseless message that forms itself out of silence.

Once for each thing. Just once; no more. And we, too,
just once . . . But to have been
this once, completely, even if only once:
to have been at one with the earth, seems beyond undoing.
                              —Rilke, *The Duino Elegies*

EARTH ELEGY

NEW POEMS

STUBBORN

Today I am offered (on my knees in the dirt
tugging)
        tough roots,

rhizomes let to stay in the ground
years
        braided and conjoined
as they multiplied, budding off the mother root
each torque of root
               anchored in earth
wedged into the very chinks of stone wall
whose base they bordered.
               Brown iris.

In the spring pungent
as lace worn near my body's close
beds and crevices
           their blooms
bearded, lit
from within, streaked gold, the petals

a mauve
I call *victorian* it is so decadent
a silk
        held up against
the bustle and flounce of the purple
most prefer.

             Brown even in the pouting bud
a stain so mordant, so mortal

that until now I did not see
under
        to the root that sucks
the wild earth (good earth, stubborn) in.

EARTH ELEGY

Rain on the shingles, on the maples—
this evening,
               ground fog and cloud
mingled in the hollow between the ridges,
and a sorrow so gentle it could be

the mud I took this morning into my hands,
lifting it
              from the garden's slump
of soil and rind, from its cursive sprawl
of blackened vine, turning the garden

after hard frost seared from purple
to black
              the last cosmos.
I put down the shovel and took the damp
earth into my hands—

and when I broke the soft clay open
found
              this twist of root
left out of last year's harvest, sown over
in spring, refired in the kiln of summer.

A hardened crust, nearly hollow. A blind
bounded thing,
              so singular
nothing might divine it. *This is my body
broken*—once a sentence of breath

spun so vividly round I could put it
on my tongue,
              and the words would
halo and hallow and blur my descent
into the barrow of unknowing

each moment is. No words now. Only this

root, humped
                like a burial mound
and the hush of wondering what to pray,
knowing full well I have not loved

I have not suffered, endangered, or enjoyed
enough of this world
                        to relinquish it
for another only made real by dying, or by
living in the holy world of words, apart

from what they point to. Here now, just
beyond the window glass,
                                evening grosbeaks
gust and go. On the sill of the quiet rain
I put the root, and I sit with it,

into the night watching and waiting,
letting whatever words come
                        go off
on a spool of breath—until, silken
and sudden, from the pith

comes forth, nodding on its stem of dawn,
this day,
                unfolding itself
into the dark like a lily. And I sense
the quick of it, so tenderly nearing

it brushes aside its own icon screen
of bloom and root,
                        black and gold—
and I am, crown to bole, just this sun
so recklessly arising.

HARVEST ELEGY

The sun rises into itself, pale gold.
Rising with it, the whole valley—
far hill of gravestones and hedgerows,
houses, paved walks, streetlights,
streets. You have gone out early
to walk the hills, the blue ridges
of shale and thin soil rising
in a clarified space that closes
the distance between us. Sun turns
the window bright amber—it flares
in the ridged veins of my hands
washing this yam, scrubbing it,
scouring this last of the harvest
to a shine with the palms of my hands.
No dirt on the root now, none
in the shallow eyes, none in the nick
my shovel gave it—the yam so keenly
polished it might be amber, a mirror
cleared of dust, or the mind
I think I want when I sit tenaciously
to quiet my thoughts, to kill them
really, forgetting to let mind be
mind, turning as it will. Now more
than the root comes to rest in my hand,
shining—the whole earth of it
rising with tamarack, hemlock, black cherry,
nurse logs, dense sprays of arrowy fern.
And just where earth meets air,
here and there in the shade, the clean
smell of oil oozing up on its own,
that smell you love, breathing in with it
those endless afternoons of your boyhood,
the roustabout and rowdy energy
of an oil boomtown, its swell of profit
and plunder so easy to deny—all this
I let rest in my hand. Finally able
to feel these lovely woods scraped down,

scoured to a final stump. These hills raw
in rainlight. House after house emptied
of breath. Blackened rivers. Eroded fields.
Distant cities left empty or razed. And god
knows what animals, birds, one species
an hour vanishing—this earth
a breath for nothing. Not even this
light left to rise in gold and hinged
shadow through the bare, black
trees.
       Remember the veery?
full-throated? how we listened, at rest
in the field, grown light in our bodies?
Doubled notes, descending in harmony,
lightly. And just look at me now,
standing here at the kitchen sink thinking
my way toward love, learning to distinguish
harvest from theft—my mute
imperfect hand closing over this yam
tightly, more tightly closing, afraid to let go.

   for David

SOLACE

I never understood   the protestant protest against
flesh   though I tried at night   to blink away

the blossoms of the tulip magnolia   my own breasts
even the stars   I tried to imagine *nothing*

Even then   too stubbornly anchored in body and mind
I parried emptiness away   The earth was promised us

Born as a slurry of gas and gravity and dust
evolving wheel   whirled out of a black and boundless

field   earth was core and mantle and crust
buffed and chafed and quickened by wind and water

Earth was rain forest   savannah   field   and hive
of winter shive-lights   Earth this raw upsurgence

pumiced by sun   by salts and chemical dusts
and tools   Earth beaten to dun mud and agon

I tried to imagine the earth   blown like a seed away
into a ghost of air   But surely (I thought)

the honing edge of the earth's long orbiting
about the sun   would leave a trace

If only a shining thread   a broken mooring
As in the fields when the mists lift with morning

and ghostly cosmologies   tremble on the wind
between whispering stalks of dried weed   And then

I remembered the birds   How they see the routes
of countless other birds etched on the rolling air

Traces as evident to them   as wagon ruts in roads
as hoofprints in wet grass   as railroad ties and jet

trails   So many etched lines on the palimpsest of air
that surely this earth   reduced to its least

would continue   If only as a melodic line lifted
from its own scored surface   A hum as evident

as a meteor's sounding whistle as it rips its seam
into the furrowed soil of the sky

And this thought gives solace?

GRIEF

Because no words can bind you to me
                              I go outside
looking for that shivery cascade of light down low
          along the roots   in the first green

of April wetlands   I settle for
mottled flecks and sparks   bloodroot   trillium

the reedy trill
of the chipping sparrow on the billowy shadblow

Let them say in purer syllables what I cannot

But look   the spring brook   flashing god only
knows why   brings back last night's rush of stars

persistent fire
                    flung from the wordless Source

And here you are again   tucking a cascade of mute
lilies into your black hair

And the energy that tirelessly upholds mountains
wild and free
                    lets words come into me

now that you are here to receive them   But first

this slow rain into the trees   this slow
rain   into the riverbed of my upturned palms

   for Connie

RIVEN

When you left, I went back to Thunder Rocks,
down the ridge off the eroded trail
through narrow ravines of cold air,
following light as it sank into the earth,
drawn to the essential heft and mass of stone
towering above me, sheerly huddled.
Winter in the stones. I wanted to get closer.
I wanted to see how the nonchalance of stone
carves space into a labyrinth deer thread through
at dawn, into channels wind flutes through.
I wanted to see how stone takes the shape
of the hull and lifted bow of a ship, possibly
Phoenician. Then to erase that figure.
To see the stone as stone. Stone riven
by the coil of root ascending into the ashen
light. And not call the cleft nave of stone
cathedral. And not think of the angel
hidden in my body, the one you wouldn't see
as the wind filled the trees and our bodies
flared in the moonlight. I wanted to stay
in the quietly resounding afternoon of stones.
And not see you huddled into your coat
on the bus to Buffalo. Already you were
back in the apartment where your wife
before she died hid notes to say she loved you.
I wanted it to stop snowing. I wanted to touch
your hands, without our gloves on. You who love
things in themselves. Long silences. Towering stones.

ELEGY TO A SCULPTOR

When you are dead, John Spencer,
      dwelling in the turning
rind of Cuernavaca's tierra firma,
part stone and marl and branching root,

I will not be content to remember
meeting you within the wall you made around
      the churchyard at Los Reyes,
in a light that deepened
                              as it spilled
through the swaying eucalyptus,
making shadowy flowers at our feet.

I saw the vein pulse blue on the back of your hand.
I saw the smear of pollen on your coat.

Back in your studio
I knew there would, still on your plate, be
yesterday's crusts, on the table a jug of lilies,

a thick yellow dust in their throats.

How hard it is to live, you said—and I heard,
how hard to love.

Lord, another baffled man afraid to love,
I thought—
          still taken up

by my own musing on Quetzalcoatl,
          so dogged by desire,
wine-drunk and spinning in his cape of feathers

he catches fire,
               in the updraft
his ashes changing to birds, blue tailed and cinnamon,
citroline,
          crowned starthroats in the pyre of dawn—
love is
          of such a nature
                    (Eckhart said)
one changes into the things one loves—
and was he then restless?
                    Or content?

Wanting to believe in love so lovely
it can turn the ragged edges of my wanting
into lines of words
                                that pulse with
the wings of my breathing,

I need to remember
the butterfly gate you made,
hinged wings of wrought iron between walls
            that hove around
the *sanctus* and emptiness of the churchyard

at sundown—the light
at such an angle
                                that even the fire
shut up in stones
burned as bougainvillea burns unfurling in the air.

And I need to remember your grief
                              as you
muttered against that philistine Texan poet,
his property adjacent,
who'd cut down his trees,
                    a stand of *ahuehuete*
whose braid and falling arch of branch
you wanted as counterpoint for your turning wall.

You loved those stones
more than memory marriage flowers wit or bread.

You loved me
                    because I loved your work.

And you, what are you working on?
you asked. A moment of confession.
I said nothing,

               nothing to say,
content to watch your gate in the burning dark—
Good,
you answered finally.

                     Something will come.

When you are dead,

           John Spencer,

I will stand by the memory of your wall,

obra escultura,

           stone by stone, breath by breath

your labor transformed to a bounding

        rush that could be

water unrolled from a height above my head,

stones tapering low, enough

to step

         easily over—then

sinuous, swooping on a tidal pitch,

unfurling, furling

serpentine, soaring in a spiral—

as plumed as Quetzalcoatl,

             as indigenous

as mountains flung towards firmament and curved

        space, held

to earth unresting by the force at their root.

Over your wall I imagine wisps of purple
on a smooth plane,
wisteria, passiflora
                    riding the tidal pitch of stone—

until I have it in me to contain
            what comes in a rush

unbidden, held
at the lip of each moment, then flung outward . . .

arbol, galaxy
                spiral etched on the wings
of the invisible moth that burns

holy, holy, holy
                    red on the rim of the sun . . .

PRAYER ASCENDING
PRAYER DESCENDING

God, let me be a sensual
hush, wind
that ripples the olive
leaves, nests
in the lush frangipani, its blossoms
scattered, crushed beneath my sandals,

lifting into flowerwine and gravid scent—

for whatever I know of source
and ascent,
                    blossoming forth,
lies rooted in the backyard plum tree
I climbed one summer night,
no more than eight,
                              and no one, least
I, knew what I climbed down from,

ripe with secrets
I want to have a word for now—

as if night sky and years of light
could be so
easily swallowed,
                         eaten, owned—

God, like a plum.

Or, if not hushed, then taut and thrummed,
as, lightly at mass, el domingo pasado,
los guitarras. Listening,

I took the host,
                    the solar disk
into my mouth,
I swallowed the sun—

                    this is my body,

and beneath what Spanish I knew,
the tree of blood inside me
shimmered down to the oldest prayer,
Maya Quiché—

> *Pardon my sins, God Earth.*
> *I am becoming, for a moment,*
> *Your breath, and also your body.*

IN THE RETREAT HOUSE
OF THE VIRGIN GUADALUPE

WANTING GOD

In the season of afternoon rain and red flowers
breaking like blood from the stones
at Xochicalco

the motherhouse shade of thick walls
is a prayer
I enter body and mind,

                  alcoves and adobe pots
flush with fern.

I sit down on the rim of a fountain
in the inner courtyard garden, a sun of water
nesting in the earth.
                Wind rises,

wind turns
the tree of flowers into a rain of flowers

and a flower falls into my shirt
between my breasts
feathery—
              and now a shudder in my hands,
like a dowser's on the forked stick, wild

with the pull of water.

PRAYER TO THE VIRGIN

Tell me, Guadalupe, you who are
another name for the wild, for the whole, for the wholly
other and most intimate
maker of souls,

                how you took God
inside you—

so that *virgin*
means
         let the fig tree root deep
in the motherhouse garden—
means
         yoke within me

this night sky seeded with stars,
this earth pressing up on
bone and vulva
as I sit crosslegged in prayer.

Tell me if to be *virgin* means to graft
God to God.
            To feel push through

from the scorned and wretched gut of the soul
flowering branches
            gold with pollen.

DOWSING

I take the flame red spray, the wild, uncalled-for
panicle of flower that grows
on the edge of the ravine
                    and put it into the opening
of my shirt, between my breasts

and go on walking over the stones and eroded
earth of La Colonia de Tenochtitlan.

I remember someone else's prayer and make it mine—
Forget your life, God is great, get up.

Let me hold these words, Guadalupe, long enough
to know
            whoever lifts this scarlet
from the open folds of blue cloth,
whoever feels this stalk of flowers warmed by my blood

is God,
            as I am—the bare
field hushed in rain or raised toward sun
also God.
            And the great emptiness
into which the sun, burning open, wells

and wells.

WANTING GOD

Wanting, too poor to offer more, I let instinct
turn inward
              to a dream of light that can't be contained
within me, that spills

onto adobe pot, fern and fountain, altar cloth,
the hem of my dress—as in Vermeer's *Girl Asleep*
how the Angel,
              lover or herald
whose head I imagine wreathed red, wet with fire

has shimmered off,
the door behind the sleeping girl ajar,
                              only light
left lingering on doorjamb and lintel,
a play of light
on the plate of fruit, light in the empty glass

before her on the table's richly rumpled tapestry.

And inside,
              inside her dreaming,
what harvest, what wine is she savoring? Her face
flushed, a little foolish.
                      Her hands curled
tenderly as leaves in a gentle wind, before the rain.

AT THE RAVINE

Within the interpreted world of stone
walls and a bougainvillea trained to bloom
into the body and beak of a bird,
exotic plumage kept to hand
and rooted, you have pointed out
the prickets of epiphytic bromeliad
kindled by early sun in the spreading tree
across the ravine—candelabra,
you say, smiling to recall
how your mother, new to the language,
said *candle bras*—and so
the conversation rambles into a thicket
of resemblances, nothing singular
but ourselves, and we hide our light.
We have binoculars and two books
to tell us the words for the birds we may
see across the ravine, the land
on the other side gone baroque
with erosion—red rock in twists
of arabesque, open sky, thin pasture.
Nothing stays, nothing keeps us
steady. A white horse dips its neck—
it's a swan. Swan drawn by a child,
faint cirrus and cumulus,
body a cloud propelled across the surface
of a pond in whose depths, as I remember,
the child has drawn the feet, black
and churning, passion and muscle
translated into act—more
exact an emblem than Rilke could give
for the love a woman
feels for a man she can't have,
going away from her, his body
far horizon, ripples of ridges
and hills receding into rain, and yet
the wick of her still burning. Burning.

Look now, you say, *just there*—
and I find the tree as a flash of gold comes

steadily to flame, ripe red
and mango, preening, its back streaked
black and white: clearly oriole,
immature form, none
other like it in the book, we decide.
I lean over the wall, over
the ravine—*barrancosa,* glad to be
warming my hands, reaching across
to a moment of sun embodied, fleet.
We have, seeing the bird,
seen each other, passionate and detached
at once—the way one can take
what comes, love it fully, and setting
free say, yes: *Icterus sclateri.*
Oriole. Magnificent. Yes.

BLESSING

For months, like a miser counting gold,
I hoarded that first day
in Tepeyac—the market of souvenirs
and Day-Glo saviors, yellow
tarps stretched wide enough to catch sun
and lift light from us. And the *milagro*
I bought, flat tin painted gold,
replica of a woman's life
given such clarity
she might wear it lightly on her skin.
And the sun, whose haloed
arco iris rippled like oil on water
into the dirty air—much too bright
for me to see in full detail
what, wanting to know you, I could
not see when you stood with me
in the hushed *capilla,* both of us
close enough to touch
that woman in her flowery shawl
standing flush with the altar rail,
her one coin held like a rising sun
between her fingers, her hand
a sweep of sun and rain over
the body of her man,
over his closed eyes, over nose
and ears, lingering
longer at his mouth, the coin
an arc of light along his shoulders,
down his arms, over back and belly,
a dip down to his groin, the coin
now so blessed that she can,
touching last her own lips,
let it fall
into a basket nested in the fire
of candles. I watch them shimmer.
This memory ripples off into luminous
emptiness—I do not know

where you are, or how, as I write
to tell you, what? that tonight the moon,
full as a prayer wheel, falls
branch by branch slowly down
bare cedar silhouettes to the wet
skin of the pond, giving back
the gold of a day elsewhere given.
And, bless you. Simply that.

CHAYOTE

Cuernavaca, 1992

I must have wanted to be here,
in the barrio, a stone's throw
from city center, beneath a sun
smeared pale across an urban
husk of sky. I must have wanted
to see this woman sweeping the dirt
before her slumped *casita.* This
boy shooting marbles into a circle
of dust. This sow penned
by a fence of rusting bedsprings.
And these huts, tar paper and tin,
that wait for the sky of sun
and acid and exhaust fumes to pour
its afternoon mood of rain into
the open drum of water in the dooryard.
I must have wanted to see what
the decent people, *gente decente,*
farther up in the hills keep out,
their solid walls embedded with
broken bottles beneath a disguise
of bougainvillea and plumbago.
Cast only leavings and mottled strips
of eucalyptus, the family goat
will take months to fatten here.
And that turkey, live and molted
to raspberry scales and lice — months,
too. Bare feet on the dirt, a child
comes to ask for *dulces,* sweets,
and I fumble into my pocket for pesos,
soiled currency — as rose and green
as mangoes and guavas heaped up
into glorious mountains in the market,
as the flowers for sale there,
lush thickets to which I feel myself
drawn, remembering how dawn lifts
shimmering in a wind of wings heard
above the jacaranda. Before she can
close her hand or draw in her breath,

before I can ask her name,
what's left of daylight flashes
its long tail, jade and silver—
and I'm remembering the warning call
of the Inca dove, translated
in the field guide *no hope,*
no hope, words too
forlorn, I thought, for such odd
cooing, barely interrogative, hardly
a warning—but the cadence moves me
over boundaries and miles to roses
I've seen on restaurant tables in New York
or long-stemmed in shops, so many
dollars a dozen—shall I trace them
back to the export fields this child
was pushed out of? I do not want to
think of that earth turned
from corn and beans to dust and thorn
and a residue of poison in petals
the color of blood. Or think
of birds, migrations of parrot and macaw,
clouds of *amarillo y verde,*
birds that no longer return to
cities like this one whose air
stings the eyes to tears. Nor
hear the chitter of their ghosts
in the hollow of this child's basket.
I wanted to come here. I said
I wanted a few images to take back,
a tree of flowers from whose branches
doves would be soaring, searing
the air with a fire of their own
creation. But here is a child
who will not look at me, and day
so dark now beneath sundown's
widening compass of cirrus and horizon
I can't see her face smile
or frown as she turns, leaving me
alone with this slim taunt of moon
as it rises through an awning of chayote,
green tendrils grasping for anchor in the air.

IN THE SWEET GRASS HILLS

REQUIEM

For the time being, earth and sky.
For the time being, body.

For the time being, nights of magpie blue,
mornings of salt white clouds winging over.

For the time being, eagle.
Eye to eye with the sun at noon,

I enter these hills of sweet grass,
sage, wild rose, and rock—

bringing nothing with me,
            a wild solitude in the smoke
                        I please to call my soul.

HIEROPHANY

What shows itself now
is wind,
            a wind
one-eyed reason, deficient in its depth,
cannot see
            as it spins
from the hub of these sweet grass hills.
Exhalation of bear,
swift elk, eagle—
            a wind
ruffling even
the lichen skintight on the living rock,
whorling now to a hum in the ear
                        as it bores

inward, bores
eyes to open sockets,
the planes of my cheeks to bone shale.

The wind says, Bow to the skull.

WORDS IN THE WIND

I bow. Now I know
what I know.
But back in the cities,
among others, would I want
to wear these hills
transformed to gold
about my wristbone?
Would I blanch the land
with cyanide and water,
mining the gold,
more in love
with the scalding light
that once
was a threshold of birdsong
sweeping east to west
beneath a shadowgraph of clouds?
Would I river
with the wind over
the wounded ravines
and scarred buttes,
over far-flung fields
eroded, that once were
thick with wheat?
And would I be happier
wearing the scant
gold leached
from this ancestral rock?
I would be wearing the people
who tell us
they *are* these hills.
Chippewa. Blackfeet.
Assiniboine. Salish. Cree.

I would be wearing them
about my neck.
And would I mourn?
Would I remember
this smell of sweet pine,
thickets of furzy flower,
and the long grasses
Sam Windy Boy gathered
and braided for use
in the prayerful dark
that purifies the heart?
Would I think with the heart,
no longer one who roves
and ravishes, moving on?
And would I learn to be
content, returning
over and over
to the same ground
sanctified by the time
being of rock cairns
and quests, by aquifers
that feed the fields
that feed our children,
by the wind that shimmers
into these hills, their brief
abundance and musky
fragrantness released
into the four directions?

REQUIEM

The wind drops low.
      Across the haunch of the hills,
            for the time being, a startled doe.

INDIAN GRAVES

I practice leaving my body
lifting above the bed
and the huddle of my body's
warm breath, rising
as the woods open—raw limbs,
and now birches tilt
through satellites and stars.
I can see through
the rift in the river of stars,
through the eye of the trees
threading east along
stone walls jumbled over,
crossing Main Brook where it splits
into shadow, long shadows
lost between ridges—new wilderness
where once were fields, foundations
wheel ruts, roads.
I keep a sharp eye out,
hunting what no one owns, no one
marries, no one wants,
following past the brook
where it turns and runs deep, hours
sifting the dark before I find them,
piles of stone humped up in the moss
and running cedar and lichen,
round mounds too randomly placed
to be remnant boundaries
or fence lines—Indian graves.

The ground is cold, corruptible
sacred. It was their custom
to sit the dead down naked on the ground,
without weapons or baskets or food.
Perhaps there was chanting,
then the stones mounded over.
I will want to sit down here
and look up into the wordless

petroglyphs of stars.
I will want rain and driving snow
and wind to lash me—pinned down,
forced by the naked will of it.
Who gets up will be lighter than I am,
more fleet—for the dead
own nothing, they practice
the strictest humility, bone
against earth, stone against earth
years of rain softly
following stone and bone into the earth.

You will say, in the morning
when I tell you this, *You were dreaming.*
I will touch, in my pocket perhaps,
a peel of birch bark. In the fireplace,
held by andirons that take the black
silhouette of firebirds,
a split of oak will have smoldered
under, a fine arched ridge of ash
along a border as white and gashed
as birch bark. I will
sit by the lair of the fire
and hear you out. You are sensible.
This is our house, our dark land
of shagbark and birch and oak,
and these will bend into the wind
as you speak. And the sun will blur
into white sky, spreading over
the sack of the deep abyss—O why
be afraid of this—sky so
burnished and comfortless and near?

CORE

Bald fire, clear as an eye,
the sun insists—this dawn
a clarity so unflinching
I endure its ferocity only
by seeing how, into its own
translucent copper, light
cuts an edge, then inks
the east ridge blue, the river
gaunt, a washed-out gold.
The sun insists. In its stare
I strip down old stories
as far as I can get to the core.
Not the goddess of harvest,
but the black hole of hunger
she tries to deny. Not
the serene apostle who knew
the Word at its source,
but the one who had to press
his flesh to the wounded
flesh of a god he had not loved
enough, breath by breath.
I hear him stammer, *my God,*
the way a hand with a match
shakes striking fire. So this
is madness, I think. My own face
eye to eye with another's,
and in that one a chink
through which the Absolute glares.
Bald fire, clear as an eye.
Nothing stirs in the field ·
but the shrill of one cricket.
Here is the simplicity of pain
as pain. *All right,* I say.
I will. Will what? I watch
until the sun withdraws
in blood. But the day isn't
done, not even in the dark.

Before sleep, I wake to cries
I can't name or number—owl,
small mammal, hungry animal, own.
Enduring their final ferocity
only by going eye to eye with
each torn syllable, until
there is only darkness. Blazing.

SYCAMORES

Perhaps I love the sycamores
along whatever edge
of bottomland, creek ledge,
town avenue, or river path I walk,
because I did not love
my grandmother,
who sucked her teeth after dinner
and offended the laws of the house by being
no less selfish than anyone else,
just as pious, and none
the wiser. I watched her
brush her knee-length white
river of hair each night. I watched her
coil it back into a loose braid and deliver
herself to prayer as a child
would, kneeling opposite me beside the bed,
and quickly,
because it was cold.
I heard her mumble *bless*
and *sin* and lost the rest
by wondering
how hair knew how long to grow
down her back and then just
stop, no need to cut it. Perhaps
something in us, wise or unwise,
just says in a small voice,
Don't. Or, *I can't help it.*
Or, *I won't.* I don't know
why I didn't love her. And she loved
sycamores, I come to learn—too late
for any reparation,
and the bond my also loving them
might make
seems flimsy. Love
for its own sake takes years.
And is hard. But just look
at those trees—each limb rippled like hair

unwound from a braid—their rare
undaunted ease
of just being. Branch by branch,
a gnarly veer. Late to leaf,
patchy white. Then a reach so sheer
it carries the eye
beyond its own uncertain radiance, or grief.

CROSSING THE OHIO
AT SISTERSVILLE

The ferry's old wood railing warms
beneath my hand. Across the river,
sycamores, crows. From where I station
myself to watch the crossing, the sun
drags its net through a shoal of jewels
alongside starboard. Summer nights,
tongues of fire, kingfishers, dragonflies
crest and ripple through the holes
of the net my mind makes—or despairs
of making. I know there's a river
in my wrist, only a fool tries to catch it.
But now I'm a child's scissored line
of paper cutouts stretched like a seine
across the river—thinking, now I am
everywhere at once, pulsing on slippery
radiance, as close as I can get to
God's eye, to the river's whole gold,
at flux and at rest, surface and source
met in a ripe confluence. And I'm happy.
Of course by now I have shut my eyes,
floating off in afterimages of the river.
But then my mind slips through a loop
of its own and quiets. The ferry's
engines strain. I open my eyes
to the sun on three tomatoes left out
to ripen on the picnic table near me
where two old men play cards. One slaps
his cards down, laughing. Streaks of gold
in the green tomatoes. And on the weathered
platform, a stain of oil so fully ground
into the grain of the wood, any thought
of rainbow iridescence slips below
the unfinished surface so many
have stood on, witness to the river.

CLARITY

When I write down, in a word,
what I want continuously
and impossibly to be—
illumined—I see how
slyly other words,
ill and *mine,*
appear, silent figures
against a ground of mist.
And I see the chiseled
profile of a woman's head
proudly affixed to a barge
Norsemen row up the Seine
to Paris, a dirty village
they think a citadel to sack.
Serenely she smiles, ideal
and visionary. They put her
before any actual experience
of light they may have
in heart or mind stored up
from their labor on the river,
with its muddy borders
and thick uncertain mists.
Wanting to believe she can
see ahead to treasure
or danger, daily their lives
become the shadows of what
they imagine she can see.
Now I watch the mist itself,
how it rises on a cry of pain
I take to be a bird. It's near
dawn, the sky is clearing—
clear enough that I recall
a friend who honors
the Infinite so strongly
he'd want to sculpt
that figurehead in crystal,
matter so transparent

it was seen by the medieval mind
neither to begin nor end.
Sheer emptiness. That is, all
presence—as it is, illumined.

SO ENTIRELY VIVID

All day I've walked the hills,
riding the curl of them
into the night, still unable
to grasp the fresh riddle
of sycamore, barred owl,
hawk on the wing of the wind,
barrow moon. Nearly home,
I pause for a long time
beneath the chestnut tree
across the street, its fragrant
cones long since tamped
into the earth by rain,
the smirched petals sucked
into the long roots that buckle
the brick sidewalk, each brick
cast with stars that bear
me up. I look beyond the dorsal
tilt of the rooflines,
beyond wind-mazy maples
and their tangles of xylem
and emptiness and phloem
to the stars we have linked
and called Orion,
like a flowering branch that spray
of exploding densities,
arching—so entirely vivid
that I receive the sky,
I take it in, I let myself be
lifted into the coal blue
ground of knowing I am
the breathing
space in which earth moves,
the time in which earth lasts,
the love that gives it life.
From here, lifted up, I cannot
help but see the earth is
not a glossy blue-and-white

celestial plum, suspended
in emptiness, only there
for the taking—but an eye
serenely looking at itself.
    Serenely looking.

TO SAY NOTHING OF GOD

Fattened all summer on wild raspberry
sarsaparilla   pond lilies   Bedded down

at noon in thickets of laurel and witch hobble
its pelage a rufescent shade near hazel

the rough boss at the base of its stark
crown like oak bark   the stag

sensing me near   may have then pressed its head
to the ground in camouflage   its antlers

branches of red cedar   sharply tipped
Or the riven staves of shagbark the lightning

sheared off in August   And I continuing
to gather mint where the pond spilled

into the brook   and I continuing to float
with the water skimmers   and the clouds

And I adrift in the burr of grasshoppers
in the field lit by sun   by mourning cloaks

and monarchs   Now it's months past velvet
past rutting   and I'm wandering

the winter slopes of dark cedars   crossing
the lichened walls that rib the open woods

Even now I might have missed the buck
dead in its winter blue coat

a thick fur I wait for the wind to riffle
No sign of breath   or struggle for breath

or wound   Neither swollen nor caved in
at the belly   Fallen on the run   its limbs

splayed out   A frozen gait so like its ancestors
drawn on the cave walls of Lascaux

And in my mouth   breath of its breath   a keening
akin to the Anglo Saxon   and to the Slavic

roots of *wild spirit   beast   breath   god*

In January   I chance to find where the buck
first fell   before he gathered

heavily each muscle   each neural fibril
each stellate cell   and rose up

from the running cedar and mast and woodbine
to clear the tumbled wall   to clear that last

acre of silence   Leaving behind him   shadowy
a flurry of coarse white hair   tufts from

its tail and heaving belly   *You are not*
this body which is born   and dies

on the surface of infinite mind   These
are words rising out of me   Do I believe them?

Soon after sundown   the coyotes come
their shrill arias rising into a snow of stars

And the wind that blows   quietly   freely
without striking words   follows me

down to the buck   And the wind flows over
the flattened blue-flecked iris of the buck's

open eye   The fox and the shrew eat
their fill   I visit the buck each morning

I just stand there and look   I don't know
why I do it   One hind leg torn

off the haunch socket   flung over the shorn spine
The clean cave of the belly   soft parts eaten

the waste already shunted hot from the coyote's
anus   Wind nests in the carcass   Only a ridge

of frozen meat   pale carnelian   on ribs that curve
like the tines of a rake   These are the spoils

Before the squirrels eat the antlers for calcium
we shear off the head and hang it

by a cord from a rafter in the barn   It turns
slowly   five feet in the air

Not a trophy   not a graven image   We want
to bring skull and antlers   inside the house

To watch our comings-in   our goings-out
To turn us from daily parrying

This task and that   So crowded out of life
we forget ourselves   The deer skull

we boil gently   scraping it clean with a scapel
oiling the antlers   We hang it

white against a white wall   above a wainscot
of native hemlock   Sun and then moon fill

the windows   The antlers pattern the wall
with branched shadows   shagbark and oak

Light drifts into the curious reefs of lace
alongside the bone snout   it roots

in the feathered edges where the bone plates
meet in a line that resembles the zigzag

of inlets and outlets seen by a hawk
above the archipelagic shore   I don't know

what to make of the cribbled disk at the base
of the skull   Or the eye sockets   entirely open

And set so far to the side of the head   I can't
match my gaze with its own   I touch my face

Jut of brow and cheekbone   I touch the emptiness
these will someday circle   and the light

that will blaze   when this body   intricate
coracle   loosens and dissolves   borne away

If I should look for this place   a century hence
the Infinite focused anew   in a body

now of antler and fur   my long bones precisely
hooved   stepping deftly into the open glade

over a dusting of snow like today's   I should hope
to be graced with an attention so keen

I'd miss no creak of wood   no distant whir
on the hard road   no tilted glide overhead

in the pine grove   By then this house would be
simply a rib of stone wall   a slumped hollow

for woodsearth and bramble   This pond a mere seep
beneath wiregrass   No evidence of otter or cattail

No sign of the spruce we planted in the field
No black spikes of cedar on the ridge   Although

a tremor in memory   may lift that antlered head
toward where they grew   once Orion rises

and strings its bridge of years on fire
across the emptiness I glimpse between them

Perhaps I might then   in the luck of being alive
be grateful enough not to mind the neon glow

still sprawled across the night   Grateful perhaps
and enough at peace to sense boundless presence

in whatever space is left open   too empty to profit by
Glad for goldfinch and junco puffed in the winter lilac

And for the sumac   tall at the edge of the road
That bold candelabra lifted into lemony winter sun

I want to look ahead   and know these acres of earth
survive our human ignorance and greed   The air

still clear enough to breathe   Random stars   Staghorn
sumac   Deer tracks in the snow

And the task at hand?   To disappear
where I stand   But to stand

in near tones of hush and mist   in the early
winter of morning bottomland   To stand

in my body of ridge and pine   the sun turning
lunar and silken   And the task at hand?

To mark the trail with a thick ring of bone
slipped over a bare ripple of wild blueberry branch

Where marrow was   an arrow of air
points toward the pine grove   the barred owl's

warren of rabbits   To be here simply
on a trail deer have etched into summer earth

And to know that the ground of the poem is
oak leaves underfoot   deer droppings

bright as black beans   a rumple of lichen
on cold stone   a possum's jawbone

the teeth still sharp   And these words
a temporary blaze   a dust of snow

RESOLUTIONS

I know what winter is, today
at least, out here
walking the ridge of quiet trees,
heavyhearted and close to
mistaking for grief this snow
on my eyelid. But, *enough*—
I say the word aloud, as if it
were a prayer, and it floats off.
And if words are incense,
lasting only as long as
I believe in the next breath,
let me first take *this* breath—
that once was mist in a field,
vapor rising, whirled
by sun toward this snowfall
and magical air. Let me want
what I have, let me take
what is given to conjure with.
And when there is silence,
let me let silence be—as Keats
may have, once in Rome,
where he saw the ruined Colosseum
just as it was, transfigured,
made a trellis redly laden
with pomegranate trees at root
in the chinks of tumbled stone.
Perhaps he plucked one fruit and ate
the tart seeds out, black
and sweet enough, and spoke of it
to no one—why should he? the moment
full of its own juice, sweet
beyond tally or trace,
the martyrs and lions and spoiled
ladies long gone, the stones
simply there for him to harvest—
thrust and gnarl, slim trunk, branch
and fruit suspended in a soft wind

that may have, for all I know,
begun when a star
collapsed, somewhere beyond Arcturus.

HOME GROUND

Just now no word arises to net what the stir of wind
    says in the hemlocks above me. Not
        sigh. Not *sift* or *sough*,
            no possible syllable

enough to hold its sound and simultaneous hush.
        But I have come to catch water,
            where ground water seeps
                out the hill

slowly over stone and root, not quite *ripple*,
            this wet pulse raveling into
                a pitcher I have used
                    to hold wild

carrot and thistle as thirsty from the dry field as I am.
        I settle into however long it takes,
            grateful for an abundance so slow
                it reminds me of

last night's stars, gathering one by one, one
        more, a million—mottled flecks
            and sparks, unsayable sums.
                No one's counting

the light-years it has taken me to be here,
        each cell flashing on, off and on,
            this body no other than mind
                inflected

and now walking into the sun from a margin of hemlock
        and fern, spilling water each footstep,
            each foot bare in full sun,
                sparkling wet.

I take off my clothes, I take off my names,
and come into the chirr of the field,
into the clearing deer have
hollowed

into the hay with the weight of their bodies, so alert
even in sleep. Within the trace
of their bodies, in the crushed
grass and pearly

everlasting, I come to rest, standing still,
both my life and my death
more gladly arising
as the water

I lift up spills down body, heal-all, and hay.
On the oil of this flesh
water beads and ripples,
drawn down,

wet sun beginning to live and die in me,
brown and good, very good, and I am
soil for seed and sparrow,
bright yarrow, wind.

THE VIGIL

1993

The Vigil: A Poem in Four Voices is composed of the voices of mothers and daughters in a family enmeshed in patterns of silence and denial, secrecy and lies. On a day in October, Sarah, a potter, holds a wood-kiln firing at her home in North Stonington, Connecticut—an annual vigil that draws the women in the family to help out. Stephen—Sarah and Jennie's father and Lila's husband, Kate's grandfather—is in a hospice dying of complications from years of alcoholism. Here I have selected passages that give each woman's relationship to Stephen. For the narrative revelation of the family secrets it is necessary to read the book-length poem as a whole.

KATE

When Sarah touches clay, it opens like a tulip, her left hand
deep in the whorl of the clay, lifting that dark

inner space, that night sky, curving it gently, her right hand
on the outside horizon, steady

as the clay thins and thins, rising to its singular rim,
that edge where *I am* meets *I am not.*

I squint at the sun, hot fire hung over sea and riprap wall,
this far bell marking the shoal off Napatree.

I'm firing my own clay in the sun, and the sun's solid gold,
an old rock-and-roll hit blasting loud as a jukebox.

I'm this body reduced to bare essence and glaze,

just a kid on the beach. *She's too old to take off her shirt,*
Gramma fusses, and off goes also Grampa's,

just to spite her. I can tell Grampa's drunk—the vein on
Gramma's temple throbs. *Black gum against thunder,* she says

as he visits his dopkit again, and the flask flashes silver.
Then oil in the palm of his hand smooths over my shoulders,

around the nip of my neck, down my arms, his hands flying fast
up my belly, over xylophone, collarbone,

up and over, slipping the oil on as you'd slip off a shirt.

The vein on Gramma's temple throbs, but he's teaching me solids
and cavities, the wet sand tricked by his hand

into pediment and gable. Santa Maria della Pace. A campanile.
Santa Andrea della Fratte. Cantilevers that jut out

and fall, della Splatte. Cave temples of India, castles,
room raum rum, build anything you want, *There's room.*

Grampa fell. Not a long fall, just over the rim of concrete
in the parking lot, the yachts bobbing,

a soft landing in the salt of the marina he called *margarita*
when he laughed with the waitress in the *tea room,*

his trousers making puddles on the floor. Gramma studied a pastel
on the wall, its monkey putting apricots back in a bowl,

not a single one let to fall over the rim, out the frame,
to the floor. Home, I watched my father's jaw

grow rigid. Mom said, *No more in the car with Grampa,*
no more castles. *Your Grampa's spoiled,* like the apricots,

had they fallen to the floor, like some children, *spoiled,*
she said, withdrawing. But I loved him.

Help this poor old body to die, said Grampa,

muzzy and fuddled, passing the buck down the bloodline.
So I took him wine, sneaking it past the nurses, a red claret

stowed in a duffle bag deep enough to house a jib. *Ah, now*
it's spring, earth flows with the nectar of bees,

he said, mocking his thirst, celebrating its power,
more than physical. But he was small in his bed as a boy.

No pity, he shot back at me. *No one knows, really knows,*
what a body's for.

JENNIE

A daughter comes home to be recognized: empty-handed. The family wants it that way. She is safer without her camera on her, without her photographs of cities and their streets. What has the family to do with *Fuck you* and *No Hang Out Here* drizzled on concrete stoops in Day-Glo colors, with peeling paint and garbage cans banged in by street fights, with the git-down-time of prostitutes and pimps? Sweep it all out of sight. A man curls up under cardboard. A man goes stiff with cold on a steam vent, sleeping. A woman sucks the pap of a whiskey pint dry and calls it breakfast. A man unwraps the bandage on his foot, finding the only vein he has fit for a needle. A fruit stall opens. Dirty air films the grapes. The cabbages are stacked like skulls back home in the killing fields. Here the killing goes slower. Even the avocado, soft and dark at its pit, knows the festering heart of the human wish to die. *You could nuke that hell-hole tomorrow and do nine dollars' worth of damage,* my father said once. I spit him out of my body, too—with each shudder of my body, more free.

SARAH

Before I enter, at the door
alone and secret, I pause
for balance at the threshold,
and for breath.
I breathe slowly, a scale
of muted notes that rise, and fall,
and rise. Smells, immaculate
and sterile, tinged with
salt and medicine and oil,
swell, recede.
How bare it is—window, chair,
and the bed where my father
sleeps, his body a faint
ridge of white beneath
the cover, his head
tilted, mouth
open, hardly a stir of air
going in, out.
And the hole that is his mouth
(that used to blow a kiss, or swear
or grin, telling stories)
that liminal hollow of breath
barely felt,
is the naught that draws me, here.

I release the will to be home,
fire rising in the kiln.
I release my will to find Kate,
or stay with Brook. To hold them.
Through tears I wait until
again I can enter
what I know of water and sun,
letting myself be drawn
beyond own will—to a movement
that, silent,
seems flame—
flame and emptiness, and promise.
I let disperse
all will but this—
I have come to be with my father.
This man who has made me burn.
This man. My father.
I cross the room,
open the window, find a pitcher
for water. I've brought
yellow chrysanthemums,
as acrid and bright
as the lie I could tell for comfort—
but won't—

that Lila and Jennie come tomorrow.
They won't, and the yellow
bough of maple, leaves
about to curl at the edges,
is from only Brook.
Quietly: to resist the lie.
Quietly: to accept
what the moment, infinitive, gives.
I run water, let it
splash about the sink.
The water chills, the water grieves.
I want water softly to wake
this man who has gone from his family
so often, that the sound
of water running, gone by,
says more aptly,
Father—father, good-bye,
than anything Jennie might say,
or Lila, too numb, too hurt.
I think of the flat stone I've kept
in my studio, a round
O in its center where water sank,
drop by drop, and hollowed.
And for the will to receive

the power of water
into the stone of my grief,
without asking to achieve
anything by my being here,
but being here,
for that will-be-done
I ask. *Your father*
wears his motives on his sleeve—
my mother's voice weaves
in and out of the leaves, as if
alive only by wanting to relive
what's as bitter
as the smell of these blowsy flowers,
heavy-heads
that shudder as I move
the pitcher over to his bedside.
I laugh softly at myself—
voices in flowers? Absurd.
That's better. A raspy whisper
meets my laugh.
A slow turn of his head.
The news of my death has been
greatly exaggerated.
Aha, I say. *Mark Twain*—

let us now quote famous men—
I know the game, a favorite
of his, and it's my turn.
Let me think, I say, but I can't.
Though he turns his head
toward me, he can't lift it.
Beside his mouth, a white
smear has dried, the medicine
he drinks to soothe, to coat,
to cloak the ravaged
linings burned by acid,
blood and gall,
and alcohol,
years of it, his recent
abstinence too late.
All I can think of is Twain
again, *Do not bring your dog,*
the first line in a monologue
on funerals and etiquette—
just his wit. A special
defiance he'd call
giving necessity the guise,
graceful or raucous, of rigamarole.
But then I see his eyes.

They hold mine steadily,
a careful stealth,
as if to inquire
beneath anything said openly
whether I know what he knows.
What I see takes my breath—
there's death
in his eyes, a fact the social poise
of his manner denies—the gesture
of a hand graciously
extended—still the host of the party
who cares, if not to please,
then somehow to amuse.
I take his hand and hold on—
not too tightly,
though I want him to say
it, let death
be spoken between us, energy
summoned consciously, agon or koan,
claimed, used—*This is mine*—
and let go of, the gift given.
And not this guarded non sequitur,
this detour—the truth
of the moment deemed improper.

No matter what death I'd opt
for, myself—this is his
to shape and honor, or not—
and so love, that profound
courtesy, has me respond
simply, *How are you?*
Tired, he whispers. *Tired.*
Then he winks. The rake returns.
I'm what they say, in and out.
He likes the phrase.
He croons it as he sinks
into the lull drugs make
of his body, medicine
his merciful angel, his retreat.
In and out, the quick
trip he always promised, into
the gin mill and out—just one.
I hear the surface pattern
of excuse, *in and out,* the taboo
rhythm of the afternoon affair, a sunrise
swim—a slantwise
permission for pleasure and guilt,
wry refreshment, and no
sense of the pattern his pain makes.

How can I tell him what he ought
to do, or feel, or be? Again,
his mouth falls open,
his breath spins wide, spins down.
He's lonely as a tunnel.
I go over to the sink. Breathing quietly,
I let water run. If I am to enter
the unknown pattern each moment
gives, at least I can
enter also the comfort of water
as it takes the shape of whatever
form surrounds it briefly.
I cup water to my face,
rinse its outline, bone and skin.
I feel how lightly
water makes sorrow's trace,
not a touch unless
touch means lightly
letting go. The room's sublittoral
as a shell, clean as salt.
My father's hand flutters open,
grasps air, shuts.
Eyes closed, wincing hard—now only
this pain left to believe in.

I sit down, now finally
with him. He kicks the cover
fretfully, like a child who would
bully illness. And he says,
though he doesn't open his eyes
or give any sign
that he feels my hand on his,
After all this, what do I know?
Out the window, far
from the misted shore, an ease
of sea horn, low,
gives itself to the sea.
Again, low. And in the pause
between two notes, I whisper
to him. How every night as a child
I looked for the light
late—beneath his door—
or opened the front
door—wishing him home with us.
If he wants the release
this shyly offered truth tries
to give, I trust—I feel
I must trust—him to take it.
Does he? I can't tell. But the yellow

flowers deepen
as if they might transmit more
light from sources beyond
what we know. I feel our lonely
honesty as if it were color.
And suddenly I'm met
by the single most vivid memory
I have of him alone—in the stern
of his craft, the line
lightly held as he waits
for wind that rises with the sun,
wind that settles east, where
the lighthouse is a bright
needle, and the wind threads
round—a ripple,
ripples—and now wind takes the ready
modesty of the sail—
and yes, the joyous
shout he gives as he goes
running with the morning wind,
one with that motion.
I feel my pain, and his, subside.
Wind and sun come to meet my father,
and I hold that brightness close.

The door opens, and a nurse comes
with a basin, a towel folded
beneath it, and a smile
that wants to be tactful, but isn't.
She wants me to leave while
she washes him. I begin to defer—
but here's my father curled
away like a child from the cold,
from the dark, from the blind
sources of pain without name.
I'll be glad to do it, I say
quickly. *I'm his daughter.*
And the guile of that non sequitur
combines with the docile
truth of the offer to surprise her.
I'll just turn him,
she replies, handing over the towel
and the oil, her look reminiscent
of Lila's disapproval.
I try to reassure her,
filling the basin, testing the water
for warmth—efficient.
She turns him from one side
to the other, careful

to tilt his head back. She spoons
chalky stuff down his throat.
He swallows, submissive,
though he rucks up his mouth,
the folds of skin
beneath his jaw so loose
they crease like a ruche.
She checks the level of his urine
in the plastic bag, undoes
tubes taped tightly to his wrist,
and leaves. Acrid,
the odor of urine weaves
above us. *I hate the smell of piss,*
he whispers. *I'm afraid.*
I shiver—this is what it means
to be naked, exposed
utterly, the first and last
pulse of each primitive
moment a death, a death, a death,
and still the ruse
of dignity, though it grows thin,
thinner, finally transparent.
Carefully I place my hand
around the curve of his chin,

my cheek to his forehead,
pressing gently. *Afraid?*
I ask him to think of the sea
he loved to glimpse
just ahead as the path of beach plum
narrowed in the dunes, the rim
of the tide line rising,
the presage of a fine sail
felt in the frail
billow of a web held
taut in the salt wind
that skiffs up the steep sand—
and once again I'm a child
with my father's enthusiasm
for the sun to buoy me,
and nothing harsh has come
into this paradise—
though it will,
and how shall I say, *Be grateful,*
no matter what unmeasured
passion flames or chills?—
so I rock him until the rousing
sea slides still,
and he sleeps in the measure of my arms,

neither father nor lover.
He slips past my hands
into an eclipse of consciousness
too deep for me,
past the image of the sea
I gave him, for courage,
to follow. I loosen
the knot of the blue hospital gown
and slip my hand inside,
his skin dry as paper.
His flesh feels hot. He shivers
and sighs with the fire inside
him—an emptiness
in the shape of a flame, a whisper
of the intensity of his solitude.
My role here is to tend—
what little I know transferred
to the work of tenderness
this work is. Forgive us
(I murmur) this
day (and yesterday's doors, hard
edges that opened, closed,
and kept us separate). I massage
his shoulders lightly—remember

the basin, now cool, and the oil.
I resume the pattern of tasks—
nothing special,
renewing the water, soaking the cloth
and smoothing it, more quiet
than warm breath, across
the gray hair of an armpit,
down fallen muscle—
wiping smoothly the rough
burl of an elbow, a slow progress
down the bend of the back's
long bone, his skin a bisque
yellow and gray—the slack cheeks
of his buttocks, and the crease
between them, his legs,
the long plainsong
of thighs and calves, the cradlesong
of belly and scrotum, and the idle
penis, an afterthought,
limp as a curl.
My hands take on the heat
of him, traveling the thin lath
of the ribs, over heartbeat
and slack breath—the unsung

history of his soul somehow held
in the hover of breath I feel
moving across my hand
as I wipe the stain of medicine
from his chin. Where his skin
blazes from the pressure of the bed,
I use the oil, then cover
and sit with him,
my hand over the one of his he still
holds in a fist. I remember
my childhood Angel,
abundantly light, abundantly color.
Light gathers and turns in my hand,
over the burning ground,
here—light
brims in the room, the curtain
fills, the Angel
fits her hand to mine.
In the quiet light,
brimming, I feel
how round and clear the moment,
how fragile—light
reconciled with light, only this moment
world without beginning, or end. And amen.

LILA'S DREAM

No longer sheltering in the family and its things, I lift
   out of my body
as once, in Kill Devil Hills, I watched a cloud of geese
   lift from the winter wetlands,
one body, a lake rising into the sky

He put his hands inside my coat, his hands were hungry,
   they found my breasts
and the hard, sweet currants of my nipples
He breathed wind into the hollows of my neck, his breath
   warm and damp through the wool

No longer sheltering in the body's blueprints, its branches
   and roots,
in a gasp I leap the last synapse
across which each impulse has traveled faithfully, to and from
   the light on the surface of the Sound

and the roof of this house is less than the question
   I shaped as a child
from a stir of fear or desire
                      What is death?

A mother lifts the top from the small house of dolls, and a child
   peers in, omniscient
Tiny pans are on the stove, the beds are made, the tiny teapot,
   no larger than a nut, is singing

and the child begins to hum,
rearranging the house given into her power

The question slips with the linens into the cupboards, folding
   into the scent of lavender and mint,
the linens tiny squares, hardly big enough to staunch a scratch

Someone, no longer alive, is hovering, each breath in, breath out
that last release that fills, and empties,

the house, taking everything with it

                    brick shingle window door

And I see the space that spins within things, light and the silence
    of light finding horizon
in each facet of screen, each spoon, each cup

What is it like, leaving the body? I have wandered out of the house
    at night
as wind threshed stars from high, back-lit billows of mist
The wind rises, and falls, and rises

It is like following my own breath
without the wedding of the body, without the gravity of earth

Between walls of wind, I see a woman and a man standing in grass
    that used to be a lawn
I know there was a house there once, because lilac and shade trees
    and over there
a clump of green thick with lilies
rises next to the cement and brick foundation

And she asks, pointing to the space between lilac and the line
    of boxbush, *there* a family played croquet,
that was a smooth course of lawn the family kept for evening games
and there were tables with cloths the wind lifted at the corners,
    were there not

From up here in the wind the shore is a crescent horn worn down
    to eclipse
by the sea's endless power of recollection
The Sound is a broken line of white where it washes the rocks
    and enters the whorl of the sea snail's house
A bottle breaks against green rocks

I hear footsteps down the hall, a door opening and closing
    like the sea
My face is wet with tears

Sarah, it will be Sarah, the Sound humming, *chiva chiva chiva*
    rising from shagbark and maple,
awakening the heart from its ancient sleep

And I know what she will tell me, oh I know

OUT IN THE OPEN

1989

A RIPPLE OF DEER, A METAMORPHOSIS
OF BEAR, A METAPHOR OF MOUNTAINS

I dream of mountains repeatedly,
running my fingers over maps where they spine
and cluster. Through valleys of rhododendron
and bear, wild pheasant and deer, I near them,
empty and still, leaning over my walking stick,
my breath easing out, a shrill whistle.
At night I stare at stars, cold and still, peaks
of invisible mountains in a sky steeply pitched.
As for crests, moraines and glaciers, icefalls,
seracs, cornices, spurs—they are psalms
of a wild solitude I am not brave enough to enter.

In the long journey to be other than I am,
I have struggled and not got far. Each day
I roam the fields, and I climb. I watch
from a shiver of aspen steep on a southern exposure
of cleared field. From the ridge rim of trees—
a ripple. A smooth shade of brown comes to merge
in the fern, gathering stillness and weight,
deer intent on the grass. I envy the deer.
Beyond them, the low mountains unroll. Clear nights,
I measure the cave depths of mountains
and their peaks—then in the hour between night
and dawn, the darkest, I dream into the mountain,

entering slim as a snake through cold soil
and stone. I wriggle down on my back, my soft parts
exposed, falling through caves rank as bear gut,
crooked as roots. *Accept who you are*—
of my labors the most naked and rigorous.
Mornings, I am what merges in the mists as I rise
from these depths, so attached to my ignorance,
I think I'm exalted, more rare than the seven
wise Hindu that ride in the constellation
we call the Great Bear. Then I envy the Bear.

GREEN PEPPER

At the stem, at the breaking point,
a hard fray of cellulose narrows,
as if someone tied it off with a thread
and dipped it in iodine. Below
this point of harvest, the stem flares
to a sombrero of sorts at the base
of six green hills. This dream
of a green Southwest just fits
into my palm, planes that swell
to a finished surface of oil and wax
and silk. *Oasis, omphalos*—
the idea of water spills in.
My fingertips trace each yield
and slide of pepperskin north
and south, a surge into shadow
and line, shoulders and buttocks.
In the world of the pepper I'm plural,
polymorphous, perverse
as a play of light in the original
void.

          And you, so silent, abstracted . . .
if across the polished table I roll
this green pepper, if I call it
the philosopher's stone, will you
hold it to your ear and listen?
Inside there are whispers, whatever
you want to have whispered. Or else
the opposite—laws of energy,
a premise for desire so pure we shy
back to the more familiar.
You smile. You take the pepper,
with your thumbnail cut in it a window.
The flesh of the pepper is crisp.
Without tasting it, I know it is sweet.
And inside? A cluster beneath time
and surface, prior to it—the white
koan of seeds and stars.

GARLIC

Up from the depths
of the raised bed of earth
the stalks lift thin banners,
green in the wind.
The roots clasp the soil,
with the reluctance of lovers
letting go. But the earth
breaks open, warm as biscuits,
and the pale bulbs, crusted
with earth crumbs, enter
for the first time
air. Braided, on green pigtails
lashed to the chickenwire gate
of the garden, each bulb
dries to a rustle,
weeks later, in my palm—
husky skins fine as rice paper,
veined like the leaf of a lily,
faintly varnished with gold.
Brittle papers that flake
when a thumb pries into
the cluster of cloves, prying
in and in, pinching the flesh
of a clove up under a nail—
and the odor! redolent,
a pungency in which pot roasts
and thick stews gather,
an aroma for eggplants and sesame
melding in a rich mystic kiss,
pure baba ganoush.
Let the feckless take it
odorless in capsules—
I simmer it in wine and tomatoes,
blend it with butter and basil,
lash the curved cloves
to a necklace I wear on my skin,
cold wolf-moon nights in the woods.

I stuff pillows with the skins,
rub the salad bowl of the lover's
body nightly with garlic,
breathe it out with the love cry,
let it rise, a nebula
into starry night skies . . .
for what if Dante were wrong
about paradise, the choirs
in their circular rows—what if
the celestial rose weren't petals
at all, but a commoner light,
a corona of cloves in their thin
garlic gowns, twisting up
into wicks that long to be lit,
and they are lit, flaming up
in the glory of God—
the God of the old myths
who leans over the fence
of the firmament, beyond pale
buds of new stars, leaning
our way, toward our own
common sod, sighing into it,
raising it, his breath
faintly garlic.

IN THE FIELD

A low wind swings down the west ridge
over conifers and beech, thorn apple
and aspen, soundless
over wild lace and yarrow,
nightshade and thistle,
over haystalks and heal-all,
moving on the face of the mist—
at my feet a twist of bindweed,
on my arm a slant of mosquito,
my blood in its belly.
Shawls of white mist
rise sheer up the ridges,
a few rags left in the air
just over the low hills
and bottomland,
over a milkiness of blue
where the river loops
and coils, sliding by—
the great snake sheds
its skin once, and once
again, the river
rising ghostly in the air.
I watch a butterfly light
on a thistle, suckle, then float.
A mizzle of mountains nudges up.

I come into this solitude
where river and mountain and earth
meet a gradual sky,
where I live with the least
grass as it lifts
into the open, where mountains
float in the wind, eye-level
between thin stalks
of deer grass and hay—
into this interval of mist
and the wind's slow

tilt and touch, its blend with
the tree's own billow,
wind passing through burl
and branch and thorn,
through ways I have learned
to put an edge on time and space,
the mist rising of itself,
no striving—and I sense,
just before the slow release
of rain, coming to meet me in low
wind, as mysterious and distinct
as the scent of wild allium,
my own lift and well,
my wanting,
sweeter to me
than the fragrance of orchids.

DOING NOTHING

I balance
on one foot, then the other,
reaching in for the pebbly berries
suspended on red whips and canes,
a lush clinging. On edge,
I reach in, the hone of a thorn
not unlike the whine
of mosquitoes beneath the leaves.
I pick my way in,
as if this discipline
has nothing to do with the moon
which last night opened
red, then paled
to the pale of a petal
in a still, black sky.
Slowly I pick my way in,
skillfully, a means that
has nothing to do with
doing harm
or with harvest.

For this moment, I forget
the pain that wants to
forget pain, and practice
touching lightly.
I watch my hands learn
their way past each
edge, each horizon,
lightly, touching
until between each berry
there is such space
I no longer have to hold
back, let go, or grasp.
Doing nothing, I
no longer wait for whole
other worlds to break open,
more beautiful than this one
whose wild darkness
stains my fingers,
my mouth, my tongue.

IN THE DESERT

Death Valley, 1987

I

Life is suffering, you say
lightly and turn your back,
adjust your pack and strike off.
The sparks fly upward,
crowding the emptiness we try
to fill with quarrel, haste
and wisdom, spires and prayers,
billboards, corridors, and beds.
We're in the desert together,
split apart, impoverished
no less than the spit-in-the-road
small towns, their tin roofs
bright as knife blades
and esperanza. Wings of shadow,
black, skim over red rock
crevices where agave and cactus,
sage and rosemary tether,
sea level, in a collapsed basin
of salt and brittlebush rimmed
by mountains. We have read
the books on discipline
and freedom, the paradox of union—
and yet we neither speak nor hear
nor see nor touch each other.
I keep you ahead of me, in sight,
the road a margin of light
I can feel in my feet. I study
salt, creator and destroyer—
fill the print of my thumb
with salt, mark my forehead,
touch eyelids, tongue. I feel
body burn. I listen to the pain.

But who can I tell about nights
when the road spills out
from under my feet like water,
and fear is all I know,
the long fall to where words fail?

II

Actually, the road is a rumple
in the sheets we've kicked
to the foot of the bed, the stars
a spill of seed, the moon
dark as earth, self-absorbed—
so that it stir not up nor awaken
love until it please. I touch
my body, not yours—a garden
locked, a fountain sealed,
a well of living water, mountain
of nard, aloes and calamus, saffron.
If you find my beloved, it is written,
tell him to imagine I've undressed
in the dark, the usual undoing,
an old clumsiness with buttons.
But that the close fit of skin,
the silk of muscle and sinew,
slip from me in the way of water
over rock. Light, I balance
on my bones, a loom pulled taut,
my spine stem and root.
Imagine that along that axis
of bone blossoms shiver and tilt.
For love is as strong as death,
though it will not be waked
until it please.

III

I enter the solace of stone
and salt and bone, things
able to be as they are meant,
as I am not. *Don't go anywhere
without me. Let nothing happen
in the sky apart from me
or on the ground, in this world
or that world.* I don't say this
aloud. Shards of an old poem,
words jarred loose by walking,
they weren't meant for you,
walking with me, to hear.
Loose words do a simple magic—
they carry me where I cannot climb.
Like love, they make sense of
my longing.
                I think *wind*
and wait, stumbling in the light,
in the dark, and in the stammer
of the stars. Here dirt is red,
that cloud slate black, sky
white. Those who've walked here
before me, this silence is their
presence, this solitude their light
released. The sun rises into
itself, pale gold. The moon has
no desire to be described.
The stones do not ask to be holy.

IV

On the steep road toward peaks
named for gods, named
for the nothing we know, not yet,
I find in hard sand, years old,
the word *listen,* the writing tool
a stone. I listen to the wind,
breathe in, choose one stone,
flat, flecked with mica,
a well of stars tucked smoothly
into rock of igneous origin,
dark feldspar washed down
an alluvial fan to this sinkhole
where we rise and fall. The edge
is what we have, salt margins
and stones that pulse like ancient
star charts. I tilt the stone,
light flaring on–off–on.
Listen. I say *canyon*
and hear only quiet glance off
centuries of schist, say *love*
and look past the horizon of personal
event, a gaze at distances
no words touch. I say *soul*
and wait. The stone begins to radiate,
to pray. *As thou wilt,*

what thou wilt, and when.

V

Out of the wind
between close-textured rills
of bare shale we put down
for the night in a shallow ravine,
uneasy. Our counterparts,
the Twins, in perfect alignment
go on walking the river of fire
into the night. Orion shoots off
into emptiness, at random.
I listen for sidewinder, scorpion,
owl—dim movements
the intellect calls unknowable
and tries to know. Of nightwatch,
of bare waiting within an absence
of will this dark, I am incapable.
I hear whispers in the sand—
Consider the stars.
Like them anonymous and separate,
you are right to live in fear.
Why open your eyes at all?
I watch, as fear takes the shape
of a mountain still distant,
a ravine so near to the bone
it fits like muscle.

But then, in the silence
I hear you breathing, and I fit
my breath to yours. Not even
the mountain with its hood of cloud
is as impersonal, as full.
We breathe in and out with the stars,
in a universe whose darkness,
tangible and near, is the hidden place
where we are knit, woven fine.
Within us, this dark
broods, and breathes, and glows.

    for David

KEEPING STILL

Because I saw
my mother, tense or careless, snap the string of her necklace,
a spill of beads shooting round on the floor,

I thought stars were so—
beads that could therefore be gathered, in one place cupped,
the sky held in a single crystal.

What is as patient, as still
as that thought? I am listening to the traffic into Boston,
how it swells and falls, in the rain a sea rushing

past the dark house.
I have followed as far as I can, leaning out of my skin, past the red
shift of car lights, through the tidal dark clouds to a misting of stars,

reaching, wanting more.
Even the galaxies, restless, are rolling farther, each from each,
on the face of eternity moving, a sweep of bright cells

rinsed daily away.
My heart is not quiet. I want the faith that moves mountains.
I want the bright force that holds them still.

How can anyone stunned by the night's consolation of stars
dare say, *I have not seen what I want*—
and yet, I say it.

IN HERE

I

On her breasts she rubbed
aloe and cast me off—
all the nouns of her body *past tense.*
But we shared a common universe,
the backyard, at whose gate
she stood when I returned—
How do you feel? Did you lose
the way? And the bed,
weekend mornings when she'd
murmur to me her childbed pain.
Childhood—a dark cloth
pulled over my head.

I travel back
to a backyard dark with
spring—hyacinths,
the wind, the willows
unknotting. Inside,
the door is clasped
with a porcelain bolt. I stir
hot milk and cereal in a pan.
She's propped in the window seat,
covered by blankets, her hair
thin and white. Before
I can spoon the food to her mouth,
she flicks her wrist
toward the window and says,

It's not out there,
what we're afraid of. The moon
turns the floor to white water,
her bed and the shadow of her bed
to a boat. She pushes the spoon
aside and says to the room,
It's in here.

II

Out of the dark of her body
I emerged—it follows
that she will enter the dark
of my soul to die.
Afraid to stare into darkness
and see only dark, she gave
the womb, that slender pear,
an occult power—the tsar's
jeweled easter, a lush fig
with choirs of inward blooms,
a clock watch on surface pleasure.
I shook my head—
The body is a meditation shawl,
I said. I couldn't look
her in the face and say,
Dark I prefer—nightgrass
and wind, the merge
of water and skin,
the mind's
unbounded membrane.

Outside,
the willow flings its green lines
to the wind and into the onrush of stars.
We listen to their silence,
pitched octaves down in the dark.
They do not tell how long
we will peel away the weave
of silk illusion, the lies
we wear—or if, face to face,
we can feel our way toward
light,
the fulcrum of our fear,
and there rest on balance,
naked,
self-forgetful.

OUT IN THE OPEN

I

The first signs of your illness I misread.
A change in character, I thought, annoyed
at the stubborn frequency of your needs.
Like a dog, you snapped at strangers.
Like a child, you had me up at night.
You'd want to go outside at any hour,
and you'd go, you'd stare at the moon
or the hard shell of snow left in the yard.
Sudden things far away seemed near.
You'd fix on them, stare off. Too fond,
you'd follow me about, insist some part
of your body toward mine, just touch.
Then the sheer fact of distance wore
you out. The tree in the open field
we'd walk to—too far. No memory
moved you from the quiet you slid into.
But when your skin seemed to loosen
and slur, when it slipped like an ill-
fitting cap down toward your eyes,
I called the doctors. They tested,
I bargained, made promises, pressed
down on hope as if hope were a seal
of eventual success. I held you, talked
nonsense, and sense, tried to tempt
you with food. I force-fed you, a tube
in the side of your slack jaw. Then
the shots, the intervals, the hours.
I'd go off to calm myself, come back
to find you'd managed to pull yourself
slowly over to the wall, find the corner,
a blind meeting, and stand there without
any sign of what it was you wanted,
as if you were pulled to an invisible
threshold, as of course you were.

II

Before any of this, months before, an echo
of the unforeseen spun out of the blind spot
in my eye and made itself visible. I made
note of it, logged it in a journal of dreams,
more taken frankly by other things—a new
word, *piezoelectric,* and the fact that the bow
of a violin drawn deftly across the edge of
a metal plate shows the pattern of that note
in white powder on the surface of the metal.
That I magnified, forgetting the sand
that blew across the path of my dream, the dust
that insisted itself into all the open crevices
of my clothes and into my watch; forgetting
how I called you to me, hoarse, wanting
you to stay, at the same time distracted
by a replica of bird, long-legged and blue,
by shells and other artful surfaces that took
my fancy, ignoring the point of steep descent,
the black hole we stood at the edge of—
a dense space where night felt like justice,
and more—the sense that the bird of the dream
had that emptiness for its nest.

III

Today, putting to rights your things,
fully aware of the elsewhere that sinks
through the edges of everything I touch,
I recall that dream, in the mood for echoes.
The doorbell rings, and I open to a kid
up the street who loved you, too. Unsteady
on his roller skates, he's brought down
an envelope sealed tight. He touches
the threshold for balance, letting air out
shy between the spaces of his teeth.
The note says everything simply and right,
if transformed by the code of his spelling.
You he's drawn underneath the tree in the open
field, beneath a squat yellow sun and a deft
V of birds drawn into a distant vanishing
point beyond paper. He watches me read
and laugh through tears and praise his art—
but neither of us, I think, can think to see
the dark blue silhouette of bird he's put
in the branches of the tree, long-legged,
for what it is. We hug, he skates off
on the shifting winter sand of the road,
and for one brief moment, watching him go,
I see everything out in the open, not knowing
which to bless more—your life, life itself,
or the patterns, blind in time, we learn to see.

in memory of R.H.B.M.

IN THE WOODS

Between dreams, desperate,
I stare at the sun's slow
swing, a hypnotist's crystal.
Tell all the truth, it says,
tell it slant. How else,
walking lightly on the earth,
can I tell it? Through
jigsaws of shagbark and briar
I map paths with my eyes,
sudden openings and arches,
then weave through. Of the Tao
it is written, *Look,*
you can't see it. So here I am
looking, hooking east with
the brook, sun now a rickrack
of light on bare branches,
a screen of white silk on the sky.
From above it's not bright.
From below it's not dark.
Where then is the gate to its mystery?

I lie down in the leaves by the brook,
I fill with dark sky. And the trees—
seen from a slant, what are they
but slashes of reed, the loose
weave of a basket or cradle.
Rocking deeper asleep,
I walk the high ridges.
Granite ledges jut out into air.
Still as centuries, pale lichens
bloom, here on the stones,
the whole planet a prayer wheel.
I sit down in this thought,
unwinding myself to a thread,
a bit of mooring left by a web
when the wind's torn through.
Briar rock blossom brook—

the Tao I can name is not
the eternal Tao. But here I am,
lightly bound to this life—
and the mystery I look for,
I'll call it the new moon,
a darkness within darkness.
Watch it rise.

CACTUS BLOOMS

Out of flat green stems
as jointed as the limbs
of salty crustaceans,
pale buds one by one
swell and flush. Hour
by hour the air around
them deepens, a stellium
of red suns rising over
shorelines of dark magenta.
If my senses were other
than they are, I might
hear the horn concertos
these blooms baroquely
unfold, might see
the uprush of spirit
in a fire of cinnabar
and summer, might hear
the wind sweep through
prayer flags, translating
their silences down sheer
mountain ridges, plains,
and rivers. But I am
what I am, a woman
at a standstill who keeps
on, who keeps on
with images that lead
her eye off to strange
altars—this bloom
the ruff of a fire god
too holy to be touched.
And then I touch it. I tap
gently, once, and the nectar
rolls onto my finger.
I taste it, just this much—
and then I let it be.

for Jean

BEGINNER'S MIND

When I begin to see
only what I've said—
my breath in the air
a snow of blind
keyholes and braille—
I let the dogs loose
in the field, and we run.
In the dimness of trees
by the wall, they chase
memories of squirrels.
I follow the wind until
out of breath
I crouch down in blank
snow, glad of the burn
of cold air in the west,
the border of trees
black and still.
Even now the magnolia
has buds, brushtips
of branches that lift
into the open.
Overhead, slate blue,
clouds swift along east.
I wait until stars
come into the blue—
then the black
never nowhere a child
gets quietly lost in.
I race the wind home.
In the kitchen new buds
of narcissus,
paperwhites unseasonal
in their bowl of stones
on the sill, have opened.
But my eye comes to rest
on a glass cup, cobalt blue,
which once, a child,

I named first when I named
what around me in the room
was living. I lift the glass,
turn it slowly in the light,
its whole body full of light.
Suddenly I hold everything
I know, myself most of all,
in question.

MAKING SALAD

after Eihei Dogen

I rub the dark hollow of the bowl
with garlic, near to the fire enough
so that fire reflects on the wood,
a reverie that holds emptiness
in high regard. I enter the complete
absence of any indicative event,
following the swirl of the grain,
following zero formal and immanent
in the wood, bringing right to
the surface of the bowl the nothing
out of which nothing springs.

I turn open the window above the sink
and see fire, reflected on the glass,
spring and catch on a branch a light
wind tosses about. Here or there,
between new leaves the Pleiades,
like jewels in the pleromatic lotus,
flash. I watch the leaves swirl
and part, gathering light fresh
from Gemini, ten millennia away, fresh
from Sirius—holding each burning
leaf, each jewel within whatever light
a speck of conscious mind can make,
unshadowed by reflection or design,

impartial. Out the tap, from a source
three hundred feet down, so close
I feel the shudder in the earth, water
spills over my hands, over the scallions
still bound in a bunch from the store.
I had thought to make salad, each element
cut to precision, tossed at random
in the turning bowl. Now I lay the knife
aside. I consider the scallions. I consider
the invisible field. Emptiness is bound
to bloom—the whole earth, a single flower.

STALKING THE LIGHT

I

Where ridge falls away to thicket
and brook borders field,
I settle into a still hunt,
heavy with rest-energy,
at one with the unshaken grace
of stone. However still, I may not
win a glimpse of the shy
habitual deer, the spotted thrush,
the owl, nor be enough within
the company of things, withdrawn
to a common depth, so that I know
the halsing and singular solace
of being equivalent and simple.
Restless, my way is to rise
and go into the stand of light
between the stand of trees,
without knowing what draws me
there, within the light,
stalking it, my own light hidden.

II

But for the moment I sit, recalling
one gold-toned photograph
of Black Belly, Cheyenne—her face
a map of ten thousand journeys.
She worked in the sun,
hard work, long concentration—
of the kind no one praises
or would think to praise,
work too necessary, too close
to the body's survival, a discipline
that's made her skin craze.
I study her burning solitude,

her disregard for pain,
and try not to compare.
If there are wordless histories
we share, I let them come
to common focus in a split seed,
beech or oak—by root descending,
stalk ascending, riven.

III

Whether I stalk or still hunt
or simply walk, I take with me
these guides—old Black Belly,
whose steps are slow,
and the split seed that opened
for me the root of *glad*
and *glade,* a shimmering space
that spills here and there
among the trees. I also call
to mind a young Vietnamese
who walked into my life
with a sunflower on its long stalk
as his walking stick, who taught me
to count and to breathe
so that within each step a fresh
breeze rose. I'd go alone,
but my solitude spins me
in circles—I read compass
and moss and the wind all wrong.
Rivers seem to flow backward,
known outcroppings fade. I lose
my bearings, pressing into
the illusion of getting there—
somewhere, anywhere—
on the long way up the tangled
ridge toward sun and open rock.

IV

Walking, I dream of that pure land,
Ladakh, bare rock mountains,

gravel slopes, bare sandy plains
where silence and light conjoin,
and all things are backlit
by the Infinite—Kangri La,
a stupa, a sandal tree, apricots
spread on a flat roof to dry,
a stone—things justly placed
in a mandala imagined for so many
centuries it's there. There,
a quiet shift of light moves
mountains. There, I lay
all my books into the stream
that flows down from the mountain
and watch words rinsed of their
griefs and hungers.

V

The wind makes the sound of hours
in the trees, a flash of sun
between hemlock and beech
the only blaze that marks
the lower rise. Higher up—
a flare of mica, ribs of birch,
a skin of water over rock.
I collect the names of the lowly,
my companions—self-heal,
hobblebush, fireweed, frail sedge—
flowers close to green, colors
that do not carry, mountain
surfaces that resemble the worn
weave of prayer rugs.
When the wind comes at me
blindside, I give up the search
for a home here, become
properly alone. Walking,
I push up from the earth
and feel my weight. Mass
after mass, the mountains heave,
holding firm. Somewhere,
hidden by all this light,

part of it, the planets
fall freely, traveling as straight
as they can through curved space.
At the core of what I am,
in that sacred space, light
does its work, as it will
without my consent
or blessing—and better so.
I climb, and the sun climbs,
at midday abundant, brief.

IN THE MOUNTAINS

In the mountains, I listen—
tracing the way
mountains arch through
air without effort,
without artifice. Out here
I can almost understand
how mountains are
words said
at a height—actual
sound made manifest
as silence, a summons
I try to imitate
setting these words down,
keeping low in the power.

This morning I give
whatever slender means
I am—an eye without
self-pity, without anger—
to the lift of sun and mist
across the surface
of what seems to be repose,
to the mountains,
to the great standing-still
of thought
to whose center I feel
myself drawn.

Around me, peak after peak
the mountains circle,
the air thin and clear.
Not one leans out of itself
into next week's sun.
Not one sinks
in my regard,
diminished to a stone
I can pocket

or keep in a bowl
with the rocks I collect
on the ridges as I walk.

In this pause, I ask to be turned,
circling the mountains
on a scale of wind and sun,
until I am once more
down on my knees at the lowest
rise, where the spring is,
listening, able to tell—
as the mountains flow
without flowing,
as the spring deepens
and stills
beneath its own precise
ripples and rills—
who breathes, who abides,
who rises, standing still.

RINGS OF FIRE

I

Deer in the field, a lucid morning,
no mist—the air clean, brisk
after last night's thick rain.
Uphill, apples hang in an eddy
of wind, dawn red, august gold.
Summer in the field, for us,
is closing—you left quickly
and went in town to buy new locks.
I relax into the detail of the day,
packing china, foodstuff, books—
housework as meditation, housework
as power—I the very wry
and proper instrument to lead
us all from chaos. Efficient,
I summon St. John, who saw arise
new heaven and new earth. I bow
to Brother Lawrence, Paracelsus,
and the physicist who put God
where God belongs,
in the detail of the universe—
albeit a universe randomly
holy, discontinuous, unevenly
plucky with photons and stars,
spontaneous. In no time
I'm in free fall,
weightless in the rift
between what I am and what I know.
As above, so below. I empty
shelves, fill boxes, label,
and flee outside, into the field
of goldenrod and fern and hay
where, invisibly, updrafts rise—
spinning rushes of wordless ascent
hawks open their wings to—
into the silence.

II

We have seen the field in full moon
and no wind—a perfect
equilibrium, soul at a standstill,
white as milk—and felt
indifferent. We've seen the field
rise like an ocean that's swelled
all night to get here—and continued
yesterday's arguments, bitter
and wrong. Just once I saw a book
left outside in the field,
spilled open by wind,
pages beating into wings
until high up, higher,
absorbed by the shining of the sky,
I could see through book and bird,
a bit of gold aloft in gold,
hard to find. So would I burn.
So would you.

III

The crickets chant *chi* and *chi*
and circulate the light—
invisible Chinese sages. I smile.
Lower down on the slope, in grass
like new spring chives, I measure
the distance to the mountains,
space across which a message
might fly—Come home.
Sun's hot on my jeans, my sweater,
and my face when I lift it
to the sun. I'm in sunfall—
a wind of light that sweeps
downhill as the clouds race,
touching first the crest,
the apples, hawthorn,
hayheads, sweet grass,
yarrow, this body and beyond—

a sweep of shade, then sun,
in so swift an alternation
that I think I can—I can—
have nothing, want nothing,
and be glad.

IV

Into this clarity of light,
into this ring of fire in the field
you come—here almost too magically—
and join me in light so bright
it must approximate (so I've read)
the last of the visions released
by one who's dying—space
like light rinsed clean after long
hard rain, a sense of sun
redoubled. But when you touch me,
the book of the future closes.
Here there is light and shadow,
hawk and wind, my nipples,
your tongue, apples, aspen,
mountain, stalk, bare skin,
the plane and sweep of bodies
moved to touch and hold.
Love is clearer than thought,
as strong as air and fire,
as the ocean of wind in the trees,
as sun in the strong green grass.

V

From here there is no milkiness
in the mountains, neither on the ridges
nor in the field. The valley
is explicit, frankly green,
the line of the far hills and mountains
precise—they are where they are,
what they are. At that horizon
I see how everything stops, full

and clear, beyond it nowhere to go
just now. No mountain to cross,
no river, no road. Turning home,
we're home already, at rest in
the visible. I see this field,
this widening circle of sun,
light so bold I cannot see
the subtle world that exceeds it
and enfolds—once,
in a dream the blue sky opened
wide, and night with its other
million suns spilled through.
Even now, they are here.
When we touch, joining silences,
we travel in their light—
with earth to write our words on,
water to soothe, fire to quicken.
The wind breathes light
into our bones, turning stars
into power we can touch, impulse
we can follow or tell, teaching love—
for that is what we are.

MEMORIES OF THE FUTURE
THE DAYBOOKS OF TINA MODOTTI

1986

Born in Italy, Tina Modotti lived in San Francisco and Los Angeles, where she worked in silent films. She was a photographer in postrevolutionary Mexico in the 1920s, a companion to Edward Weston. As a nurse and a member of the 5th Regiment in the Spanish Civil War, she worked with devotion and commitment, a woman who had learned to live single-mindedly in accord with principles that put her on the side of the poor and the oppressed.

Her photographs take essentially ordinary objects or working men and women as their focus—a field of corn, the rims of wineglasses massed together, doorways, streets, markets, a young Mexican reading a newspaper, hands at rest on the handle of a shovel or washing clothes, telephone wires, workers carrying bananas or crossbeams, women with large gourds on their heads, puppets, Mexican street children, a still life—stark, iconographic—of a hammer and sickle against a muted background. For years lost or neglected, Modotti's photographs have steadily gained recognition and are being exhibited more widely. In 1995, a comprehensive body of her work was exhibited by the Alfred Stieglitz Center of the Philadelphia Museum of Art. Modotti's photographs communicate a powerful dignity and simplicity and integrity—qualities of Modotti herself.

History retold is revised history; biography relies on intuition and imagination as well as document and fact. *Memories of the Future* is neither biography nor history, though rooted in both. *Memories of the Future,* as a book of poems, is a creative revision, an indirect translation of the life of Tina Modotti. The poems are drawn from daybooks I imagine Tina Modotti to have kept during the last years of her life in Mexico City. In fact, she did at times keep journals, and she wrote a poem after the death of her first husband. And so I imagine her in 1941 writing prose entries in her journals in one of the small rooms on the fifth floor of Calle Dr. Balmis 137 or on the *azotea* of that house, from which she could see the city sprawling out toward the horizon and the volcano Popocatépetl in the distance. Made more solitary by a serious heart condition that was to claim her life early in 1942, she writes in the spirit of *querencia,* a gazing back through the distance toward home, remembering the times she had shaped a new life for herself or had it shaped, in postrevolutionary Mexico, in the Soviet Union, and in the struggles in Spain in the 1930s. I have "taken" the poems from those imagined daybooks.

MEMORIES OF THE FUTURE

1 January 1941

I've heard it said we choose our own deaths.
In all the chaff that fills us, the clean seed glows
and will explode at the right time.

That seems a pretty thought to put beside a corpse,
rude comfort—a hot-water breakfast
for a hungry child. There are men who live
wistfully dead, wanderers who walk the streets
gently beneath a smothering blue. They put on
their clothes in the morning, remove them at night,
put them on in the morning . . . For them
to choose to die is a birth.
                  I know a different dead—
those the fascists shot in the working-class streets.
Drenched in oil to kill the smell, they were left
on display. Women swollen with child were forced
to drink petrol, men to dig their own graves.
Their wives had to watch, wearing signs:
I married a Bolshevik. Did these die at the right time?
And the wounded, slowly those with no breath
left to come gasping in bubbles of blood—these, too?

If we choose our own deaths, we choose all of it—
the kiss of our parents, our bodies, doctrines,
dark rooms. All of it our will. As an immigrant
I saw the coastal horizon move toward me, a clear
green line. I signed my name there—yes,
I said. I will be . . . and I chose it. Then moment
by moment I remembered and forgot as the future
moved toward me, through me, past—dimly, then
more dimly remembered. We choose our end.

But when we get there, do we know it?

I wanted a life plainly used, transparent. The ones
close to me, could they not see? Seeing,
could they not know more than I could in words

express? Silence is nearest to trust.
Now since the war in Spain,

                    alarmed by darkness,
heartworn, I tell each face that invades my sleep,

Join love and power, then you can never be hurt.

Once I thought,
into the poverty of darkness the moon casts her lot,
radical, beautiful. Our lives can be.

DOCTRINES OF GLASS AND WOOD

5 January 1941

In my memory, light shifts distances about,
faces wash in a shimmer of light that's not sun.
In one of these memories

the wind furrows deep
sea channels out to the open sea. Papa's there,
the ridges of Friuli and Caldori north in the distance.
We turn past Venice, past a cemetery wall, toward
islands, villages, boats bobbing like bits of *cristallo*
on a sea glass backed by silver. Above Murano
smoke from the glass factories hangs low.

I recall
faces in an orange light of furnaces,
clay pots like beehives, a water trough, and balls
of fire rolled, pressed, cajoled and tricked into fine
docility by enormous men. Fire doesn't die—
it is the glare of strong hearts. But it can be thinned.
I watched Benvenuto—my uncle a hero—take a gather
of glass from the molten pot and blow, and in three blows
a red pear grew on imprisoned air. It was a dancer
stretched, an orchard of myriad things, all possible—
then rolled on a marver, thrust on a block and blown
deep red into a mold, and clamped there. It set
a moment only, and when the mold was opened, there—

a globe . . .

taken by tongs to the lehr for its slow journey through
that tunnel, annealing with time, a tiny world
deceptively cool, taught seemliness, given limits,
made single—an individual thing, and real—
or so it seemed. But Benvenuto mocked the mold.

The glass was on fire, he said. *But it wasn't free.*

Intended for the tables of the rich, the glass might be set
like a helmet of breath over orchids and pearls.

It might glitter at the Savoy, a hotel in London
flooded once so the guests might eat as if in Venice,
floating in imported gondolas while jeweled black men,
like sconces, held fire up on thin glass candlesticks.

Benvenuto told me this—he was a set of lungs,
a set of muscle. No more? Perhaps, he spat,
an alchemist on wage.

What did I then know of anger? I was six. I saw
glassblowers shape with their breath glowing forms,
each shimmering sphere like a life. Into the light
by their stems I wanted to hold them, glass
after glass blown for milk or wine or the hours—
a cluster of roses, transparent in the light.

Of me alone, Papa asked,
Who are you? What have you done? What more
can you give? For whom are you poor enough?—
until the questions had dignity, and my life,
which was to answer in work, had a chance
at dignity, might build something new.
He was a carpenter, these questions
his plumb line and rule.

As a child, I was his partner. I cleaned his tools,
I walked with him to work, to look for work.
In the midday trattorias he hummed violin, I danced
on the bare wood table, a tiny child buoyant in
smoke and sunlight, in the smell of sweat and basil
and bread sure of the sane, undemanding love
I sensed there, a strength basic as polenta,
natural as rain.
        In him I saw the power
to build—in brick and stone and wood. I learned
to wonder how a man could do good work, the work
required by others, and feel betrayed. He was hurt
by work, and by the lack of work. Who respected him?
We never framed that question.

FIRE DOESN'T DIE

7 March 1941

Yesterday I was drawn
by this season's first light rain to a café
on the plaza. *Salud,* said a stranger, pausing by my table.
He sold me a rose and a small round of bread. I smelled
the rose, I ordered wine—a glass for myself and a glass,
as is custom, for the unknown guest who might,
out of the hubbub of guitars and parrots, come sit with me
and be still.
    And then I saw, firm as memory,
a fine mirage. Robo *presente!* He was squinting, confused
by the uproar of Fords and crowds, *presente,*
stern and vague, with his usual book, the one with blank
pages, in hand. Almost I said, Sit down—we'll take
wine together. We'll drink as before.

But he would not sit,
and I grew cold remembering the formal portrait
Weston made of him—a stance theatrical, hands
elegant, half Robo's face in shade. He'd cracked a door
so that he stood composed in a triangle of light,
a telling slant of light on the floor. The portrait
Robo held out for me to see shook in his hand.
He placed it quiet on the table, tracing over and over
that triangle of light with his thumb. *The two of you
are lovers,* he whispered. *There's confession in the light.*
A little sad, he smiled. *Look here.* And it was true.

He turned even more to his paints and easel,
to mantras and blank pages in so blue a light
I couldn't follow. He wanted private horizons—
Facts are not always beautiful, he wrote.
He wanted a world of rare delights in which beggars
gave their crusts to bright birds. By nature,
he couldn't possess. I was his glass of red wine,
sipped gently and gently set down. I was the rose
on his coat, admired. Worthy, but without
knowing why.

I wanted to be more visible—to see, to contemplate . . .
but I also wanted lilac wet with morning drawn
round and round my taut nipples. I wanted
the mystery women make with their bodies,
blood and milk. I thought I wanted freedom—
but I wanted to be used.

Primavera in Friuli, I was the last to notice
first green, blind until all the grazing field
swept tidal, sea-fire green, though the shoots
one by one had been there, gathering force
since solstice. Just so, until the afternoon,
alone with him, when Edward spilled sake
on my upturned hand, and took my palm—
bending close as if to read what that shudder
in my lifeline said, and put his mouth there
instead (a pool of rice wine warm as semen,
clear as a lens) and drank, and my hand fired
like a cup in a kiln—
                    not until then
had I noticed how our casual glances one by one
had gathered to such a steady gaze that California's
hills and fields outside swept to full kindle of vine,
the sun a green blaze.
                Robo was asleep
when I came home. No eyes to look into. Papa
felt near, just a notion of him there as I walked
about in the room, touched the pears in a bowl,
the shadows in the chest of paints. I lit a candle
in a dish. I stared as flame split the dark,
split it sheer. A chasm opened,
and I stretched my hands to its light—in part
to warm them, in part to block the heat—
then raised hands and arms up over my head
in the spire divers make as they arch . . .
before the plunge,
                a moment's hesitation,
balanced on the edge of a depth so pure I seemed
to choose, without sounding it, free fall into fire—
swept by fire.

DOORS, OPENING AS THEY DO

27 March 1941

I think I ought to begin to do some work, now
I'm beginning to see . . . Robo left these words
on the kitchen table, Rilke's words copied in black
and gold script—an apricot, unripe, set on the page
as a weight. Join me when you are ready,
the apricot meant. Elegant words: *One ought to wait*
and gather sense and sweetness a whole life long,
a long life if possible. If possible. I began to see
a pampered man, that Rilke, a silk smoking jacket,
a mauve cravat, a table of mahogany mirror
in which reflect many cities, men and things,
a surge of wings, and a heart's blue iris, the petals
unwinding in slow pirouettes. Beyond his window
laborers like Papa sweat, while on the other side
of many white rooms a woman has her life
invented for her—white, white.

One must have memories, many nights of love . . .
and childbed and deathbed, windows never shut
against wind, a long spool of road to unwind through
bright hills, the sea in storm, monumental skies
and stars—in short, one must live.

A week in Mexico, Robo wrote how doorways,
opening as they do from the public street
into gardens of green willow and wine bougainvillea,
charmed him—such intimate exposures he wished
for a door in his chest—he'd let a lover in
past the veil of fruit trees to watch three gulls
carouse at the lip of a well, and that well
a deep door down to the sea. A man could drift,
casual petal down that well, and float for centuries,
the centuries could float in glass-bottomed boats,
we two alone with them, reviewing undersea roses
and the arbors of bone and the light that rises
from such bone. That same light shimmered
from the page as I read. I called it his despair.

Then he died. He didn't see cities collapse
into fields, and the fields smear with rumor.
Younger than I he remains,
                                    leaving for me
only a moment on the train when a telegram was put
into my hand—I was going to him. He'd died,
it said, alone, the final words on his tongue
blurred in the heat, a page torn from his journal
tight in his hand. So they said—
I never saw, except in dreams, that door swing
open on its hinges to the empty chair by the empty bed,
the plants in their clay pots unwatered.

Once there in Mexico,
in the young afternoon only hours past his burial,
I stood on the street at a doorway, looking in.
I let doorjamb, threshold, and lintel frame
a woman on her knees patting tortillas.
Like butterflies her hands moved soft, her courtyard
savory with earth and lime, soaked *maíz* and woodfire.
Between one *maguey* and a loop-eared cactus
chickens scratched. Her man stacked *ollas*
for the market. It was all there:
one moment, shining, impersonal.
I wanted to hold each detail. I wanted time
to stand still. I wanted soul to be sun
as only the sun can be, warm in the murmur
of doves, fresh in the folds of a just washed, pale
yellow coverlet. The moment passed.
She stirred a pot of beans, he finished work
and sank into siesta against the wall, his serape
wrapped around him like a wave from the sea.

That moment I was apprenticed. I was changed.
I went home to learn the camera, back to Weston,
changed. I would bring him to Mexico. Meanwhile
on the train, I slept in a homely smell of milk,
warm tortillas in the basket at my feet, across from me
a *campesina,* her bundle of child slung tight in her shawl.
Out the window,
                        tierra caliente: hot land, blue hills,

sun like a giant *comal*. And in my dream, a woman
held a ball of fire in her hands without pain or harm,
bending over a vast bowl as she shaped the fire,
squeezing, as if she were washing a towel or
kneading dough on a heated stone, Indian-style.
Though her eyes were blank and blind,

she showed me the work I'd chosen.

FAST LIGHT

5 May 1941

Last night
on the *azotea* I watched the west of the city
flash and burn its fiesta—cannonades,
mescalito songs, great wheels of light
that dye the midnight orange and rose. Madrid,
I thought, Madrid! the street in flames, days
and nights on my feet, in the hospital stumbling
about the kitchen and the halls stripping sheets
and the dead—anything not to sleep,
anything not to dream.

I remembered Edward. In last night's splendor
he'd have seen only a rain of stars—
and they were there. In Mexico, as anywhere,
the dream has mists of gold to envelop you,
and you go in gold, arms outstretched,
to feel your way through pyramids of onion,
chiles, papayas, *aguacates,* white walls
of calla. For you think the tree of life
has tumbled from its distant constellation
down in a tropical rain—more fire
than rain—masking hills with green and lupine,
filling lakes with hyacinths, clouds
with lilies. In this ecstasy you see
mere silhouettes for the men and women
who daily go in grief to the vendors of small
white coffins in a heap. Or you see that wood
and call it the natural pruning of a primitive life.
In Mexico, the rain of stars can be
the sting of sweet evasion in the soul.

With Edward,
                    it was fast light, sudden twilight,
darkroom nights. Between living and dreaming
he loved a whitewashed solitude
to which I'd run barefoot in the rain,
my kimono open. The room would fill—a cot,

an old wool flowered cloth, blue jar, fine light.
In the slow, slow thrum of our bodies we'd come,
whispering, *I'm not moving, not moving.*

I'd wash prints at noon, and sense . . .
something amiss. A beggar's gaunt face,
that could bring the mood, or the cluster of
roses I'd arranged, four buds unfolding in stillness,
clitoral—the body's female clock.
Such riches, poverties—either one
might thin in the chemical wash of the tray,
so much less than I'd meant. Then I'd quit,
I'd help cook, I'd lie in the sun, sealed off,
a stone. *Estoy un poco triste hoy*—"I'm sad,"
I'd say, and walk the *avenida* with my Graflex,
drawn to doorways, arches, stairs. Where
did they go? inside, through, down.
We are born in shadow, we live in a mist—
but I couldn't break through.

Afternoons in a glare of light impersonal as history,
I walked. I watched whole lives disappear.
Men and women of the barrio, they'd turn a corner,
miss a stair, enter silently a warp of air.
They weren't missed. So many of us have done it—
stepped over the drunk in the street,
turned away from the beggar on whose sordid red
stump a splurge of flies swirls like a dance of filings
drawn to a magnet. Such men have no future—
simply, they don't exist. *Whose world is this,*
I said. *Or mine or theirs, or is it none?*

And where did I live? In Edward's room?
in the street? In my own room I noticed
first, in dreams, random images—
in a yellow light I'd never seen I saw
a crowd of corn, notched bamboo, a mass of
sombreros for sale. Above a clot of huts on a hill
clouds lifted, weights that might fall
on a world too still to have people in it yet.
There was a contour to the silence. I knew

the streets would fill. I'd see their faces.
In the center of this pueblo there was a public
well, a rope to sink down it, a clay shard
near for drinking. The town might change—
should change; would.

I waited for the streets to fill.
But there were only a few baskets, red chiles,
reeds—no hand to weave them round.
In a window wind rasped the dried roots
strung there. Sometimes I heard numbers tallied,
like the names of the dead after battle.

Awake, I watched the sunlight. Slowly I began
to fill it. I photographed the corn in a field,
bamboo—each crowd of it weighty, real.
Each had a bruise of shadow, each was a refuge,
quiet.
                What I felt . . . I couldn't say it—

Why am I in such despair?

DARKROOM NIGHTS

7 May 1941

One night in Amecameca's Hotel Sacro Monte
I lay awake—the bed hard, the pillows white
with the geranium and stock we put there.
Mountains cold, moon aloof—Edward
shivered as he slept. I couldn't close my eyes.
I watched a chair cast ribs of shadow on the wall.
How well they kept their secrets, I thought—
the things of the world mute, patient.

The bed was a lumpy altar—
I had been worshiped there, lifted out
of myself, by the ecstasy of my specific female
flesh made goddess of the flowers, flush and open.
I was able to stop time, back to the first time
we'd touched—let it be always the first time,
Edward said. Sex is magical thinking—
water burns, flowers dawn in the stones.
The first time, in Glendale, he'd looked at me
first through the camera: an hour's delay,
glance as touch, and finally, finally touch—
a slippery transit, beyond all limits.

Was it magic, or skill, when he took me
naked on the *azotea?* in the sun shooting finished
photographs—decisive, my body a figure
of Aztec craft, every curve and cut made
with love and power joined in sure design.
I had a dignity delicate and fit.
Yet I'd dread it when he'd say,

                              Come, Zinnia—
I'll shoot heads of you today.

Those days I lived as a man—that is,
wore jeans, smoked a pipe, refused to make
vows to my lovers. I was a willful solitude.
A doctor had said, *You will never have children.*
I could make no appeal—the doors in my cells

slammed shut. My body sealed, a tomb. I appeared
to be, and was not, a woman.
                                    I lived in the darkroom
of my body, mute of all light. My body had
betrayed me—or had it freed me?
I wondered, do we ever invent our lives? We yield,
or we rebel. When are we our own?

That night I waited for the moon to sink to dawn,
a glimmer of the irreconcilable just beginning
in the backlighting of my brain.

In the morning we climbed the volcanoes. Below
stretched a mesa of level green and blankets of water
where hyacinths floated, above them clouds
of infinite muscle. I saw everything to scale—
how small we are. My questions hushed.
What I thought I was, I wasn't. What I thought
I knew, I didn't. What I wished to do,
I couldn't. I was single, a moment
alive in skin and bones,
simple seeing.

IN THE MARKET

1 July 1941

Today on the street I ate a sugared coffin's
sugared child, and in one swallow Guanajuato's ground,
like a gunshot, opened. I was back in the Panteón
I'd toured with Edward, back with the dead.

I can't think what made us go.
With the taste of coffee still in our mouths,
we'd made love. With the straw pattern of the *petate*
imprinted on our skin, we'd washed in the sun.
Down the steps to the fusty vault, I felt his semen
leave me, wet on my thigh. Why would we have wanted
to see bones? That is, I'd expected bones,
not bodies warped in tight skins, in brown
naked hides. Not the scythe of grins, all flesh
made rind. And not the pod of a fetus with its empty
suck at a leathery breast. Edward said,
the ultimate still life, a monumental theme.
But I heard the baby smack its lips, and I fled.

I found myself in the market, touching onions one
by one. I traced silhouettes of shoots and calla stalks
on air, watched one bud split its caul and the white
spathe open. Cold, I let street life slip over me.
I searched each face, in each heard a dry, deathly
smack of the tongue. But I realized for the first time
power—the power to see a world buried in daylight.
I was a lens—and I saw.
                There rose up for me
that day in Guanajuato's streets the dead and the living—
they breathed through my breath, they rinsed through
my pores their blind needs. They were hands
scrubbing clothes, they gripped shovels
and newspapers, lifted cones of bananas, carried
crossbeams on their backs. They went down in the mine
to a source like their mother—they danced in the dust's
brief abundance. Together they endured.

In the street a man shouted a drunken *vacilada,*
hermetic pain pulled inside out, mystical
and snickering like a mescal worm, laughter
that stabbed at the light. *Los muertos mueren,*
y las sombras pasan—"The dead die, shadows pass."
But the air they breathed, we breathe. Their faces
backlight our own, our lives spring up
from their dreams—light
in the work of these thick city streets.

In the center of town I saw
an old rusted pump the color of ocher,
color of bloodstone, ancient as the channel of the vulva,
menstrual color. Near it an old woman in a black
rebozo stacked tortillas on a cloth, a *brasero's*
charcoals glowed, and the old Ford motor
used for grinding the pueblo's corn chugged along.
There was a smell of oil, smoking meat.
I remember the water's iron taste—I used
two hands to pump it. I drank from a gourd.

I thought of lilies—how they pull water clear through
their green channels. In them was presence,
an ease of future. As for me, watching dark water
splash in the dust, wiping my wet chin on my sleeve,
washing my hands in the earth-colored wet—
I'd have struggle, *la lucha.*

VOCATION

16 August 1941

Me considero una fotógrafa y nada más.

"I consider myself a photographer, nothing more."
I said that in the years I lived alone.
The words gave me focus, purpose. I never believed
the words. Subject to the violence of *things,*
the bourgeois man makes claims—I am *this,* or *that,*
or *this*—and he lives in that cramped prison, alone.
I lived as one free—a photographer in the morning,
communist in the afternoon. Nights I kept to wash
prints, watch stars, smoke and read. A silent time
to count gifts, the best ones
                                danger, disillusion, failure—
gifts that say what you are, how you must
continue.
            Today, my birthday,
an old friend brought back to me old negatives.
We held them to the light. A child at a brown breast,
the technical focus: nipple. Other children
hungry in the dust—born empty, moved through
empty rooms to empty dust, to live or silently
die there.

My friend said, *These are the best of you, Tina*—
as if they were not children, but old skins
shuffled off a former self, as if we see
only ourselves when we look
"out there."
            In the negatives I held, I saw
children remain rooted—but I am the child of departures,
always the immigrant. What next? the unexpected.
What more? the loss of wanting to be more.
What power? longing.

Who is content to be witness only? Sometimes my chest
burned, urgent. I'd think then of Mama's patience
and carry it, rain in a bowl, to the darkroom

where I worked.
                    In Tehuantepec
campesinas carry on their heads wide gourds
painted with flowers, broad as moons. They glow
and wither and give seed. Rain fills them up—
in drought women walk to the river, the sun
hanging gold in their ears. What they know

as they wash ash and dust from their bodies,
as they fill gourds, and lift, and bear them home—
their feet falling sure, on dirt roads
retracing the steps of their mothers—what these women
know, *that*
                    I wanted. I wanted to walk to the river
in the company of women powerful by nature.
I wanted the burning well in my chest to flow,

and someone drink.

DÍA DE LOS MUERTOS

1 November 1941

Today, shadows laugh at death's circling
and at sexual longing—all hunger.
How fat is the city?

                Fat. It lolls at crowded tables,
wears gunpowder, facepowder. Men who should be
massing their power . . . dance, until fat shakes loose,
their bones unlock. They dance *vacilada* and laugh—
and death returns it.

Nothing is lost, years ago Mella said—
his head flung back, his blood in the street
like a dare. Nothing is lost, I believed that.
Though for days after, my image for life
was a woman drinking wine from a funnel,
her feet inevitably red with the spill.

Was nothing lost? Still Mella lay on the pavement,
the wind blew. No sirens, but the moon rolled down
the street in a state of shock, the moon tumbling through
all its phases, full to new, like a broken clock. I ran
from car to car, from house to house. Mella bled
in the street, a man strolled into the library to find a book,
a woman scolded invisible children. I screamed . . .
but how peacefully he bled! his blood
sinking and joining rivers underground, the rivers
that dye corn red and feed and feed the future.
Wine red, he flowed there. Nothing is lost,
he said.

At his funeral, I was the dark one—
negrita cambuja—the one near the white stacks
of roses. Armband white, heart white as splinters
of bone in his ashes, I stood in a negative world,
no darkroom for work out of public view.

The body that had filled me, his body,
now filled an urn. Some of the ash I'd scattered

on the street his blood had stained, the rest
would be sent back to Cuba when we could.
In Cuba, the tyrant Machado sucked sugared
drinks through the long hot *tiempo muerto.*
I suffered dead time, too: time after *zafra,*
or harvest, when hands hang down and hunger
has emptied all promises. Students struck
sparks from the discontent. In Cuba they cut
cables of the Electric Bond and Share—
these spat in the streets like imperial snakes.
News of the murder thickened in the air,
a smoke of fire not ready yet to burn clean.
Hurts smoldered.

Just the day before, I'd photographed him.
I hadn't washed the blood from my skirt.
I hadn't let them tint his cheeks. I thought,
Let them see what they've done. He was cold
to touch, yet the illusion of breath-fire lingered.
Upside down on ground glass, the image of my lover
breathed stubbornly; he slept as I'd seen him
mornings. I had to shoot frame after frame
to believe him dead, identical frames, no new
angles, no tricks. *Dead* means you can't revise.
Dead means fixed. *Dead* means the stern prison
of form, beyond any love which rebels against
blunder, obstacle, hunger—these powers,
these *compadres* of the poor.

                                    Alive means water,
means assuming the shape of the glass water fills,
but first shape the glass with your own deep breath.
Alive means will. For this is political alchemy—
make water burn. Make water burn what binds us,
make water burn what binds us transparent as glass,
make water turn wine in the glass.

                                    This is *síntesis,*
among the last words on the page Mella left
in his typewriter. I photographed the words
and the machine whose keys had transported them
from his brain to flammable paper. Blank paper,
I went to his funeral. Soon they would write on me,

words of hate. I wanted to dawn—*madrugar*—
to see swift just revenge form like sun on the blank
scroll of the sea, and the sea unroll all its power
on the kill. But I was alone. I had no power for that.
I waited. I could feel only the surge of my own quiet
will redoubled. They could not move me.
They did not.

When the press called me *puta,* conspirator, spy—
for the fascists!—when they broadcast nudes of me
and said things, when they flayed bare skin
with their questions or used me like vodka,
they wanted what men of that kind always want—
a mirror for their own fingers at their own
secret parts. And when they were silent,
their silences hissed: Don't you know what love is?
Why is your uterus empty?

Don't you know what love is?

WHAT LOVE IS

2 November 1941

Most of us
can only say, I caught a glimmer of it once,
a light mere words find hard to come by, a silence
whose value rises in degree like dawn through a still sea
or like the candle lit in the green street stones when it rains—
then stone is matter raised in power, more itself.

Out the window now the moon's a rim of a polished cup,
its *pulque* poured out. Like the moon, a fraction of myself,
once I turned and turned, alone in the room, alone
in the city, alone—until walls blurred, edges
blurred. I dilated and cleared, spun round in total
revolution,
          no one to tell
I was empty or full, there, not there . . .

Then I knew how the mystic's rose is shattered, its center
everywhere, distributed like corn and beans and guns—
rosetas, by the handfuls given out.
                Any way you turn
it's one vision. When *look* is the work you do,
love is there, beyond good and evil, beyond talk—
which does not cook the rice, grind corn, or clear land.
Unless you talk this way—
             say what you really want.

When I say *life,* for instance, I mean what's possible.
When I say *soul,* I mean the material bead of rain that hangs
from the margins of a storm. I mean what gathers and fills
and depends on a cross-fire balance of winds.
              When I say
love, I mean what we've had and had to lose to be what we are.
I mean what continues without us, and somehow,
because.

MARÍA

In Salvador and China, in Spain and Nicaragua
risings began.
          Sandino said,
When the people are satisfied with freedom,
let the ants bring me the news underground.
I could no longer use a camera—no one face,
no mass of sombreros was enough in number.
I was one of a mass whose horizon I couldn't see.
I focused on the daily task. I let love
set my limits, when I could. I let the body,
whose discipline is pain, choose a generous
death.
          Now I was María,
Mexico's name for each of its alien poor.
I took the name, studied in Moscow, traveled
long roads in hunger. I said to the sun,
you lead me. Somehow a modest life grew.

We had a world, we said, to wash clean, minds
to renew. I was one of the many drops of rain
on the clear pane elegant tyrants erect as a shield
between themselves and the poor. This glass,
I felt, we will wash it clean, break through—
and if in the heat of love or hate
we dry on the glass (blood spatter, rain spatter,
wine), well, we do.
          I was not afraid.

I lived level to the need to stop blood, carry water,
make soup. Before Spain, I loved best
the work away from desks, the wordless work
of fields and floors—digging or washing or gathering
wheat in. In Spain I lived with Carlos. I thought,
he has organized an army: his will. And I can still

see the 5th Regiment,
their caps thrown into the air, the last bars of

"La Internacional" lingering in the shouts to be on
with it, a massive surge of faces, blended and composed—
tidal music, centuries of repression breaking free
at last, we thought. It was a time that compares
with music, with a harmony of will and sacrifice so valid
it feels as if the world is spinning in your hand,
and in that rhythm we moved, firm in the principles
and demands of the time, inviting our ancestors, all
those who suffered, to be there in the impersonal
intensity of our blood. We had, for a time,
great power. And as always with great power,

we were tested.

FROM A SINGLE CENTER . . .

21 December 1941

we tried to live. That's as it should be.
Now there's argument and doubt.
The center shifts, the line falls back, allies
unmask themselves, or mask. A few dry apologists
argue the war, they justify by numbers—how many
of ours were taken for *paseos,* how many of theirs;
how many cells were filled, emptied and filled,
by mistake how many; whether the ears
that hear confession now detect through their sleep,
faint and shrill, ululations the Africans made
when they fell on young women, how many at a time . . .

What is counting but the wish for distance?
I counted, too—lentils, so scarce we doled them out
like pills; children who needed succor; Franco's
columns, four, and that mysterious fifth, the spies.
By Málaga I hoped never to see another war—
and then Guernica, Brunete, Teruel, Tarragona,
Barcelona yet to come. I could, in the last year,
no longer tell the color of an armband,
so many were blood, no longer measure loss
or honesty—they are not flour that sifts or bandages
that fold. They are open wounds down a corridor,
you want to close your eyes.
                                        Lines that fled
the burning town I counted by cart and car and mile.
We had to be calm—was there time to feel?
My heart was sealed, a cask of wine let down a well
to keep from thieves, to age in the dark and cool.
Thirsty, or longing to be drunk, I'd send down
a grappling hook and hear the echo of a thump,
the scrape of stone and metal. Because I had learned
to hold a gun, to shoot, I saw in my hand,
as if in a smoking mirror or a lake burned off
by sun, the Aztec signature of war unfold,
the blossom at the tip of the detached god's bone.
You can't ask what is cruel or kind.

Was I blind?
                    In the war I saw up close—so close
a mountainside of stark trees against snow could seem
an old man's face, unshaven. A rose was an urgent
smear, red down a wall. When we had time
for a personal love, Carlos and I,
we used our bodies like braille.

Events are our minds turned inside out.
In Madrid, in heroic November, the wounded
were loaded in on stretchers, in the trunks of cars,
or slung in carts like sheaves of torn hay.
In the kitchen a cauldron of thin garlic soup,
some beans. Bread came stale—in burlap sacks
long skinny loaves, floured "bones" without feet.
Their knobs blued with mold in the larder,
the leftovers stacked there, too tough for jaws
that stammered and mewed cold breath like gauze,
then locked in a final freeze of pain.
                    María,
they called—the urge for last words so strong
that almost, almost in the conscious ones I'd see
words gather speed, change, shake free
like sweat on muscle. Nearly impersonal,
finally beautiful, they told their last stories,
their lives, keeping alive in their whispers
what never can be lost . . .

Sometimes there is no time—it cascades
and eddies, flows backward, spews future, past,
and present in a mix. In San Martín, a jolt
of the ambulance over the ruts of the field sent me
a glimpse of a face—I saw a child, gentle and sad.

He belonged nowhere, and he stood exactly there,
in the red dirt, dried garlic looped in the window
behind him, the smoke on the white walls ashen.
He held a broken puppet by a string, something
human or animal carved from a gourd. I looked,
looked again, but had to go on—to Madrid,
to beds where young men left their words in blood,

where fever smudged the sheets with visions
of their children, born and unborn, orphaned
to the cradles of the mud.

If we could look into the future, would we go there?
In the spiral of hunger's discontent, would we go?

Somehow we go. New societies are born,
much wider than our minds. And if for a moment
we doubt, our bodies remember. They believe.
We make our bodies available to death,
and therefore live. It is the hero's way—

every woman knows it.

HOME

4 January 1942

I have lived many lives since in Venice I saw
glassblowers shape to their fragile uses each angry breath.
Now the days come one by one—I predict neither
memory nor future.
                              Yet I have seen,
one twilight in Moscow, a piece of frozen river
ruffle up into the sky—ice as a pale blue rose
too distant for tether or root. I rubbed my eyes,
and the rose broke apart into whip-lines,
long arcs and Vs—
                              and I knew they were swans,
perhaps wild geese, in their mass and sheer
movement amazing. Near the bridge where I stood
were skaters. They scored solid ice, their shadows
long behind them, moving into night. Above
and below, the world moved one way.
I have moved with it. That I know.

Where is my home?
My small life has touched lives in Italy, Los Angeles, Mexico,
Moscow, Spain. In them all I see the photograph
Edward took at Tacubaya—I'm sitting in a doorway
dressed in black, in our courtyard facing past a tree
and shadows on the wall. The wind that swept Mexico
is still, the dust is low.

Edward has set his tripod at a distance by the well
where he washes each morning. I dream
sun on the *azotea,* the darkroom of a new life—
unaware of the pattern composed as he backs farther
away and stops down to so great a depth of field
that the door goes back into darkness forever.
That dark doorway I call home.

Out on the street, lovers saunter, eating celery.
Azucenas spill from the windows. Churchbells, anvils,
roses ring in a single translation. *Vivid, la vida sigue*—

"Live, for life goes on."

                  None of us has time for a single
life to stun the air as a flower can, fully realized.

Therefore we gather, en masse.

LONG WALKS IN THE AFTERNOON

1982

LONG WALKS IN THE AFTERNOON

Last night the first light frost, and now sycamore
and sumac edge yellow and red in low sun
and indian afternoons. One after another

roads thicken with leaves and the wind
sweeps them fresh as the start of a year.
A friend writes she is tired of being one

on whom nothing is lost, but what choice
is there, how can she close her eyes?
I walk for hours—either

with hands behind my back like a prisoner,
neck craning up to the sky where chain-gang
birds in tight nets

fly south, or with hands swinging free at my sides
to the brook, the water so cold it stings
going down. Either way, I whisper

to dogwood, fern, stone walls, and the last
mosquito honing in, *we're in this together.*
Here is the road. Honest dirt

and stone. Some afternoon, heading home before dark,
if I walk by mistake, lost in thought, far beyond
the steep trees, the satellites and stars,

up over the rim to a pitfall, past any memory of words—
even then I can give my body its lead,
still find my way back.

THE INHERITANCE

At night the pattern of shadow and light above my bed
reminds me of a banister, stairs and a railing.
I hear footsteps coming up. She is holding a candle.
Either it will be my grandmother with her long white
bolt of hair brushed out silk to her knees, or it is
a young girl in a cotton nightgown quietly cupping
a day-old rabbit, dead. And once more I'm there

in the house where the stairs spiral up from the hall,
the wallpaper white like cream still warm from
the cow—the house that burned, the old
country place in my mother's family.
One afternoon when the light was amber I hunted
foundations and woodsearth there and found
one china cup, white, intact.

I heard women in long white dresses, with puffed
sleeves, reading aloud from books with blank pages.
Quietly their voices crossed over each other
like braids, telling the arts of dust and milk, larder
and closet. The fire begins at the hems of their skirts,
so long they brush over the stairs, the floor, even
the chicken yard but never get soiled—

the fire starts at those clean, clean edges and scorches,
a bad iron burning as slow as their voices, pausing
only at intervals when my grandmother pauses,
staring off into space where she sees lined up into sentences
her grandchildren, her future, mute cups she must fill
with milk, with advice. No one notices the fire
crept now to their knees, to the hems of their starched white aprons.

A coal kissed my mouth—the family Bible had
a cover brimstone black. I've carried its burning

cinder beneath my tongue, long obligations of love
listed in a slanted-back, presbyterian print.
Worn at the spine, it descended
through the men in the family. I'll never own it.
Someone else's hands will mend the torn pages
with tape, other hands will tremble in lamplight,
holding a glass to magnify the words, lifting
unsteadily dried flowers a child

saved there decades back. I'll never be able
to tear out the pages, scooping them up by the hands
full, never be able to make from its sturdy black
frame a box for geraniums, cream white
the blooms, manna white.

I'll never thump it as my great grandfather did,
saying, *This is my house, and the Lord's,* so loud
the dog slunk out of the room. *Oh, everything was
simple then,* my mother said, polishing the apples
father never refused, holding a shining one up.

I saw how roundly the light curled around
it, gold. There was no dark side, no disobedience,
no willfulness, lust, or adultery, no questions,
no pitfalls, no ambition, no greater knowledge,
no greater love.

I slept in the house that burned, one hot summer night,
an infant. A blessing to have us together under one roof,
surely grandmother said that as her grown children
made their ways back to their bedrooms, the beds
now strange to their bodies and July hot as fire.
Perhaps there was honeysuckle

and a stir of wind in the curtains, then a billow of white
starch, and lavender scent, and the sheets bloomed
down. I slept in a cloud. Afterward, they said
there was no one to blame, though the family
scattered like ashes, one chimney left standing
and the wind blowing hard.

The men suffered most—a hangdog, hurt look
hollowed out in their faces. The women had children
and husbands to tend, a slow watchful working of gardens
and cupboards and the long book of memory.
The house was a touchstone, a ruby whose luster
lit up our dark corners.

Even now before sleep, the house reassembles its porches
and windows. From ceiling to gable it gathers the light
like the church of a displaced longing. I'm never content
with the facts, somehow responsible, homing
when even the birds have fled, and night
closes over, a lid of black smoke
and the moon an ember.

THE ONION

Mornings when sky is white as dried gristle
and the air's unhealthy, coast
smothered, and you gone
                              I could stay in bed
and be the woman who aches for no reason, each day
a small death of love, cold rage for dinner,
coffee and continental indifference
at dawn.
                    Or dream lazily a market day—
bins of fruit and celery, poultry strung up,
loops of garlic and peppers. I'd select one
yellow onion, fist-sized, test its sleek
hardness, haggle, and settle a fair price.

Yesterday, a long day measured by shovel
and mattock, a wrestle with roots—
calm and dizzy when I bent over to loosen my shoes
at the finish—I thought
                              if there were splendors,
what few there were, knowledge of them
in me like fire in flint,
I would have them . . .
                              and now I'd say the onion,
I'd have that, too. The work it took,
the soup it flavors, the griefs
innocently it summons.

AFFIRMATIONS

> see without looking, hear without
> listening, breathe without asking
> —W. H. Auden

I

An Eskimo shaman
will take stone, and with a pebble sit quietly
for days tracing on stone a circle,
until snow and mind are one.

Gazing into the whorl of a knothole
I sit out winter. Someone mutters inside.
Just one tremor before the walls give me
another white word for snow
this wood desk shimmers, as if wind
had reached wood's spellbound
galaxies and seen
the polestar
turning.

II

Storm coming, this sky
brews, swelters—a guttural verb.

I listen to Mahler in the darkened living room,
his tumult like birch trees, hundreds
in a limber thrashing against
black sky, light broken
from a source so electric
even the roots shake.
And in all this hear nothing
until the contralto
rises out of the swirl,
vulnerable—

and such a stillness after,
I hear water
begin to bead on the yellow sycamore outside.

III

The word *death*
lives deep in the oddly branched vines of the lungs.
It is a wind instrument with no stops, a low
whine you ignore because conversation, or the owl's eye
yellow of the sky at dusk, or the solid crack of wood
split for the fire distract and claim you.

I am learning to breathe
without asking for breath to carry me anywhere
but here, to the split-second rush before wind
strikes word, to the moment I am what I am
without knowing it.

ICE STORM

Saplings hoop over.
The pines list, steep and grave.
I want to say *gravid*.

Roofs all over Connecticut give.

Someone somewhere
must be homeless, dark, and drifting
to madness with all this glitter.

Red buds closed into clear ice
seem to swell out.
Plump, I'd say, as currants.

At night the child
I will never give to the universe
for safekeeping

skates over my dreams of the ice crust,
hurtling into all that white.

TO SPEAK OF CHILE

Sometimes, what is most real shimmers, a dark
geography of dream—a film off its reel, tangled
on the cutting-room floor. Someone edits
what we know.
                    Take Chile, where the songs
of Victor Jara swelled like a harvest—now a filmscript
of sunflowers spotted with blood, silent banners of smoke.
In the market, a car black as a tornado stops for you,
and you disappear. Chile, a mass grave in a mine,
workers like sacks of potatoes thrown down cellar.

And these are facts. If I am silent, I consent to them.
In such a silence, I could not take my own life into my hands,
rubbing its skin like an apple's. I could not touch it
with the reverence I hold for the newborn, or for the dead
bodies of those I love enough to wash and dress for burial.

Things your hands know, you respect, my exiled friend
Ulises said, up to his elbows in flour, making bread.
And if dignity becomes a habit, as I believe in labor it does,
and in the courage to resist even those who cut off hands,
a man in prison can whisper songs. Ulises Torres did.

BURNING THE ROOT

Cedar at first, then a splay of staghorn put to the torch,
it burns, a relic of Georgia O'Keeffe's, in the fireplace.
We distance ourselves from the cedar's simple wood,

shape changers, making love on the floor.
When smoke curls up one protruding sharp antler
and puffs in the room, you get up, poke the fire,

shift the root. In front of the fire, you turn suddenly,
closeup, a blue movie in my brain. You burn there,
fire licking your horn, your fine fur.

Then we finish and sleep, who knows what secrets
smoking, banked down deep. Though we fit together
simply, like spoons,

the room is a Saracen plain, cedar root turned
sacrificial ram on the spit, seen from the underside,
hind legs out stiff.

And it keeps burning, the smoke a curl of contempt
in the wind, not unlike the smoke of a cigarette
held to a bound woman's nipple.

UNWRITTEN HISTORY

> If we could shake off our individuality and contemplate the
> history of the immediate future with exactly the same
> detachment and agitation as we bring to a spectacle of nature—
> for example, a storm at sea . . .
>
> —Jakob Burckhardt

This storm won't be given a woman's name.
It has no calm eye. Nor would you call it
a mirror of human passion.

Although waves of the Atlantic pitch alpine
and green over coastal cities, and cones
of dust dance over the plains

this storm does not uplift. It cannot be
worshiped. It creates no new stars,
no heroes or heroines, no history.

In its full radiance
inks dry in their pens, pencils
flare like matchsticks, film
smokes in the camera.

In the wake of this storm, the wind cuts
as never before, straight through.
We lie down in our bones
like X rays.

Who knows how many years will sift unrecorded
or what fossils will print in the saharas of salt
where seas used to be.

From some other planet
this storm may be noted as cloudbursts
are now by the crab and the eel—
this apocalypse of ours
jotted down

as a relative movement in the cosmic
dance, an unforeseen quark.

But then
on the horizon of dream, like a nail
nearly pulled from its plank, there is
one blackened
tree.

In the dark of its inner gestation, years
collect, ring after ring of light,

a memory of men and women walking in parks,
in the mazes of fire thorn, along walls
espaliered with fruit trees. Then

over fields and highways
a litter of satellites, arrowheads, bottles, old gods.
Artifacts that whisper,

This is all they could do

This is all they learned

This is all there is

RADIATION

a liturgy for August 6 and 9

A CALL TO WORSHIP

Stand in the sun long enough to remember

that nothing is made without light
spoken so firmly
our flesh is its imprint.

Whirlpool nebula, the eye of the cat, snow
crystals, knotholes, the X-ray diffraction
pattern of beryl—all these echo the original

word that hums in the uncharted mind.
Listen and answer.

RESPONSES

If the corn shrinks into radiant air and our bread
is a burning cinder
                    like chaff we will wither and burn

if the thrush and oriole vanish, borne off in the wind,
unhoused and barren
                    we forget how to sing and to mourn

if our cities and mountains fall into the fields
and sleep with the stones

how can we leaf through old photographs and letters
how summon our lives
                    our hands will be smoke

CONFESSION

The bomb exploded in the air above the city destroyed hospitals
markets houses temples burned thousands in darkened air in radiant
air hid them in rubble one hundred thousand dead. As many lived
were crippled diseased they bled from inside from the mouth from

sores in the skin they examined their children daily for signs scars
invisible one day might float to the surface of the body the next red
and poisoned risen from nowhere.

We made the scars and the radiant air.
We made people invisible as numbers.
We did this.

AN ANCIENT TEXT

There is a dim glimmering of light
unput-out in men. Let them walk, let them walk
that the darkness overtake them not.

PRIVATE MEDITATION

(Shore birds over
the waves dipping and turning their wings together,
their leader invisible, her signal their
common instinct, the long work of years
felt in a moment's flash and veer—

we could be like that.)

COMMON PRAYER

And when we have had enough profit and loss
enough asbestos, coal dust, enough slick
oil and dead fish on the coast; enough
of the chatter and whine and bite
of stale laws and the burn
of invisible ions,

then we are ready to notice
light in the gauze of the red dragonfly's wing
and in the spider's web at dusk; ready to walk
through the fallen yellow leaves, renaming
birds and animals.

We will not forget our dead.
We sharpen the scythe until it sings loud
our one original name.

OCTOBER ELEGY

Precisely down invisible threads these oak leaves
fall, leaf by leaf in low afternoon
light. They spindle and settle.
The woods open.

Birds no longer
slide by without my noticing loneliness in the bold
stare of the night sky—a sphere
tight as an onion.
At night I wake to a cry like the tearing of silk.
I listen and listen. There is only an owl.
Again, owl. A dog barks.
A clock persists,
its parody of single-mindedness
heroic.

Then mornings, they begin in mists that lift
toward noon, but first as if you've dreamed them in a deep
breath inward the trees come shyly forward
like ribs. Then the doves,
their breasts the color of hewn
cedar, call and vanish.
No one, you beautiful one just beyond grasp,
slide your fingers along my arms
as gently as you slide down
oak and beech and shagbark
loosening the leaves.

Who's attached to you, *no one* . . . who could be?
In ordinary commotions of grief and joy
you're elusive, a radiance
that flashes so strangely different each time
or so seldom
we say of you, *once in a lifetime*—
remembering perhaps phragmites on fire
in salt-marsh light where river crossed into the Sound
or the blow of light that glanced between mother

and father nakedly, once. Just once
laying the fire, remember how I whistled,
myself entirely and no one?

No one would say this:
you may as well laugh in delight,
cut loose. Interpret in a moment's
surrender your heart.

I watch the oak leaves fall.
Surely by the time I'm old I'll be ready . . .
surely by then I'll have gathered loose moments
and let them go, no longer dreaming on the stair
sun-hazy, surely not the old woman who thinks that by ninety
she'll wake once, if a split-second only,
and live.

No one, if I were able to forget you, or find you, I might learn
to enter the cup I am washing, door I am closing, word
I am opening with careful incision, lover or child
embracing—
                    and fall toward that moment fire cracks
from common stones, a sunrise in evening.

COUNTRY WOMAN ELEGY

With a hush in their voices
country people round here tell of the woman who walked
bareheaded in winter, keening aloud,
three days wandering with her seven-month child
dead inside her. She wouldn't be comforted,
she held her loss.

Telling this
the old men shake fear from their eyes as they might
shake rain from a hat or coat. Her madness they blame
on winter, the cold and closed-in weather.

I love that woman's fearless
mourning. The child dead, no help for that,
she had to wait until her wanting to love the child
died out in echo and outcry against bare stone.
She had to walk, never mind the cold,
until she learned what she needed
to learn, letting go.

And I love those reticent men.
They know how most of us strain to ignore our dead,
the woman less fortunate to feel the weight of hers.
Who wants to admit death's there inside, more privy
to our secrets than any lover, and love
a kind of grief?

Therefore we dream.
Last night a wild, purple bougainvillea bloomed in sleep.
I thought to gather a handful, but the stalks broke
like straws, and the wind
took them

and drove them past that woman
bareheaded on the winter road, that woman whose cries
unwound and wouldn't be comforted by love or a lover's body,
by childhood or any piety.

UNBORN CHILD ELEGY

Tell me a story
                 whispers my always unborn child
and I pause, listening. Whenever a word
shapes itself outward in speech
there's a hush.
                In the beginning, I tell her, nothing—
if you can imagine nothing. Just so, and patiently, the ancient
stories begin.
                Once, lying down in the backseat of my parents'
car—their heads dark on the windshield, telephone poles
outside, and the heads of trees blown back against the stars—
I tried to imagine nothing. Warm air rushed on my eyes
erasing the car, the trees, the stars. I inched across
a bridge of thread called emptiness, cold.

Then I knew you were there inside,
asleep in one of the body's seedbeds.
I could hold my breath and find
you, small as a syllable,
a grain like pearled barley in the hourglass of my brain,
a stitch in my side.

We made a pact. I'd bring the world inside,
the moon your heart,
a dark plum your eyesight.
You'd bring me so close to the unspoken I'd shake,
some of the mystery spilling like salt.

Today snow sparks the air like mica—the sun's
just so, cocked right angles to the wind.
I bring you the snow and it isn't enough.
You whisper you want to be born.

I study your whisper, I study my fear.
You're bound to pain, my mother said.
Each child pries you open.

No one will believe
how alive and present to me you are if I refuse
you a body. But I believe in nothing, a transparent
breath from which all form and color rise
in a passion of wings and leaves.

In the ancient stories, the world begins by surprise
when zero speaks, from mere words
weaving sun and moon, the fire
the flash of snow.

Be the zero who speaks for me.
Be birth and death, the emptiness
only a child, and never a child, can fill.

GLASS ELEGY

The day she went mad, she watched white sun
emerge from the oaks, shaking loose
the dark as you'd knock garden dirt from an onion.
At breakfast, though we're just now putting in seed,
her talk ran to harvest.
                          Out here, she said, *I'm transparent,*
a single bloom in a glass bowl of water. I don't need
mirrors, I don't need field.

Later she came back to the house, scattered.
Her hands had flown from her like birds in high wind,
vanishing in a rent of air between trees.

During the worst she lost her eyes,
her ears, her tongue. The glass bowl cracked. She couldn't
recover her collarbone, her right foot, her left breast.
And because I'd learned to talk to her as I would
to myself alone in a room, I tried
to go with her, eyes shut
into the suck of black wind.

Hold still! she cried.

She'd been so long in front of mirrors,
an image in glass, a glass bloom
in a bowl—
                    and when she broke through,
the woods moved in quick, everything out there
verb, quicksilver changes. And these swallow you
unless you turn mirror yourself, and the world
flashes from you each moment.

And then she was quiet.

I can't account for her words that morning, what she later
saw, or the calm finally out of which she spoke
with such authority.

She described a random, long walk in the afternoon
when the woods breathed with her
and she lived through the power
of death and the earth's
rotation

as ordinarily
you do, she said, if you're ready to notice.

In the mirror that evening, dark branches tangled
weaving my face with their fire, and almost
I could reach through and touch the ripening

long sweep of wind toward morning.

GEMINI ELEGY

You are not here, I cannot touch you, or be still.

I walk out of the house to watch the stars, and stay
hours after the last plume of smoke from the chimney.
Wind in his ribs, the Bear tips his nose to the east,
keen for the dawn.

I walk these ridges on a tilted light. I look for the orchid
whose blossom floats from its slender stalk, the one
the Greeks knew resembled the scrotum, wildflower
delicate between your thighs.

Through hemlocks and oaks I hear an owl cry,
low. Breath only, but it startles—like that first
forlorn gasp of hunger, pretext enough
for a lifetime's headlong desire.
                           And the stars—
every one of them speeds out of breath toward the rim, apart.
Even Polaris, even the Twins, our Gemini lovers, their hands
joined in a single star, distant
so distant their feet, on fire, walk
calmly into the River of Milk.

Even ordinary lovers suspect
they must rid themselves of desire. But to take
expectation by the taproot and keep tugging on the line
coiling it, that takes inhuman effort.
And to hang the coiled root on a nail in the sunroom like garlic,
not as a trophy but as seasoning for soup, that takes a wisdom
we require only of mothers, old women, saints.

Yesterday I planted wild iris
in the morning's low mist and woodsearth
by a shelf of rock near the brook. I felt as though I were tending
your body—it is such gentle work—and the roots,
dark threads, brushed wetly over my hands
like nerves, quickening.

ONION ELEGY

Hour after hour,
gathering wild onions from the banks of Main Brook,
I follow the old worn way of knowing the world. At first
I see simply onions, then lopsided pearls with green shoots
so forked they resemble the tails of exotic fish. Now
they are once more onions, simply onions.
My hands smell of onions, so does the wind.
By noon I am talking to myself like an ancient
herbalist who's studied, and remembers, the small preparations
old men and women make before they die. At last

they turn loose of old furniture and letters, they turn
mirrors to the walls and stare out windows, dreaming
of pod-shaped boats stocked with picnic lunches,
with books that are dog-eared, new shoes and worn
socks, the buttons lost from a favorite shirt.

Suddenly they have the vision of telescopes.
They focus down long dirt roads and find
the moment they turned this way, or that,
and a certain aroma of spices faded from the wind,

or a part of themselves they called secret
and never shared clung like beggar's lice
to a stranger's coat and walked off,
unknown.

                    They grow calm, no longer afraid. How can they lose
themselves in death? Already they are scattered. Still,
they long to be gathered and used. They are humble,
single-minded.
              Nothing. No one.
              The words still haunt.

Whenever I've failed to love emptiness enough, I fall
inward. I hold on to myself, dense as an onion,
as compact, as tightly veiled.

But today the passion to lose myself in work and be quietly
with the dying at their sunlit windows
fills me as air fills a room.
For miles I've followed
this brook in the calm the dying feel

when they put their hands
into a shaft of sunlight

raising the dust.

FIRE ELEGY

In small numbers the birds are back, one by one, new call notes.
Then by twos the tanagers, bright as struck fire, return
from their winter's ark. And others, suddenly visible
flashes against still trees.
                    Our bodies are like these birds.
On a signal so clear they don't have to think,
trusting to certain mute scatterings of stars
they just get here, and strike a beginning.

These mornings my blood rings loud, and I wake in time to hear
five and six, seven, echo on the clock upstairs—
and the birds, their cadenzas and solos. Then our outcries,
in passion the low vibrato I make when we strike
the bell of our bodies deeply—all this music
flung out of the body's loneliness.

Just now, polishing a window, I drifted beyond the smooth
and slippery loveliness of glass, beyond the soft
cloth and lemon-sweet scent of the water,
dreaming our bodies, polishing them clean
as the spring air that skims
these trees, as light

as this whispering fire along a nerve—and knew
the body's lullaby wish to be bounded and fed, joined
to another's long journeying, a continuous keeping
in touch. Why else, after long migrations, nights
in the ice floes and winds offshore in the Sound,

why else, after breaking the spell of boundaries,
do we return to each other, lulled
by the rise and fall of our bodies
coming together, on fire.

Thanks to the body
I learn my own call notes. I sing to the horizon,
whose way is to move continually beyond our touching it,

stopping, or seeming to, only at odd
intersections—only last afternoon

I walked down the fireroad that winds through these woods
to a clearing of trees and a field, just as the sun swung
its pendulum down the horizon. This season only,
at this one moment each day, the red
medallion's struck

on the crown of the road, so that every stone flares, and the fireroad,
true to its name, burns each branch and new nest,
each thistle and weed,
each crevice the frost made wide in the road—
and the sticks of my body, arms and feet, all
the bones kindle, and I burn with last light

unafraid, part of it.

SIGNS

1979

A GRAMMAR OF THE SOUL

> While we sleep here, we
> are awake elsewhere.
> —Jorge Luis Borges

While I am on the dark bus and the spin of the wheels
    carries me into the crowded tunnel

she is rigid   awake under the scream of mosquitoes
    and one lightbulb bare in its socket

While I am sleeping in a sling between two palm trees
    which rattle in the trade wind off Cayman

she is hosing the blood off the sidewalks in New York
    after the accident   dreaming it green

While I am sleeping in a field of grass making love
    with you so that she will love me

she is in the mirror where it is snowing
    she is freezing to death

When I am unbuttoned in the cold winds of the hailstorm
    or blacked out in the cone of the twister

she pours a glass of cold milk and leaves it
    for me on the kitchen table

When I am dreaming that my body is pacing in the rain alone
    and drifting in the cupboard of a strange city

she walks down the other side of the street wet and
    smiling   She does not see me when I wave

    She does not hear me when I call out for her to stop
        to tell me the name of the city

She cuts through the alley and enters the keyholes
    for she is wiser than I with secrets

While I am sleeping hard with my back turned
    she is writing a poem in my voice

She is lying behind me tracing words on my skin   words
    I will not remember in the morning

When I am pretending to sleep   my breathing a snare
    she tacks off on a reach   the jib sheet in her teeth

and thinks of heading south to a country where red
    chickens strut in the villages

When she is in the marketplace where the rabbits hang
    by their ears among strings of red pepper and garlic

I whisper how I have always been the stranger here asleep
    in your arms   restless and content

When she is sleeping with her maps and charts and lakes
    smoothed over her for cover

I am walking into the room where you are
    drumming your fingers on the polished table

While she sleeps waiting for me to leave you
    I decide to stay

REMEMBERING WHAT I WANT

Sometimes the room will darken, and I'll hear
cries I know aren't birds.
Perhaps I've just read
how sandstorms took an ancient city
into hunger so deep there were no mice
left, no crows.

Or I've remembered Tolstoy said God
was the name of his desire,
and other wise men and women strove
for the act that left no trace,
pure as the sign of geese
reflected in a still pond.

That's when I'll echo what I least expect,
much as the taste of ale or alum, walnut leaves
or sharp camphor grow
mysteriously distinct.
I'll turn to myself and say, as if I were
someone else—

How can we be content?

Sometimes the room will darken, and I'll know.
Moments like these, they resemble walking
into the kitchen to boil water for tea
and, forgetting why I'm there,
I'll watch as my hand
finds paper

and writes down what comes,
if only my name.

THE GARDEN

March–August, 1974

PLANTING THE GARDEN

Snow seeds the air

Warm in my parka I break ground
Earth gives

Clouds muscle by
A woodpecker knocks in the pine

I walk off the rows

measuring with twine
planting outlines   stake and string

I remember a grandfather
lunatic and blind

Earth he called *dulcimer*
Music he called *seed*

Asleep
he heard the echoes of roots

To greet him I traced the line
of my name in his callused hand

He called me gardener
a signature in soil

I stitch the seeds of lettuce radish chard
in their shallow lines

The moon is the owl's eye
as I finish by dark the planting of corn

I think that wings will lift from this clay

Already I see one of them risen
perfectly white

The green one will tassle and cob
But the white one

the indigenous angel

will ripen in wind no man has felt on his bones
will release from its husk a covey of birds

sunfeathered   loud
and they will sing

SUPPLICATIONS TO MAKE
DURING PLANTING

Spirit of the Garden
hear guesswork

or if questions are prayers
these prayers

What are the names of the resurrection

Whose eyes have I borrowed from darkness

Why is it easier to come
    in the gaze of a stranger

than to come in the fields of desire
    to lie down in the head-high grass

        that bodies may be wells in the earth
        that sun may draw us up

        that we may be the rain which washes
        us clean   the touch of our mouths

What are the names of the resurrection

How can the soul be separate

Why don't you touch me

Why don't you speak

DREAMING OF THE GARDEN

All day I've weeded   raked
mulched the tomatoes with straw

examined leaves for flea beetle   aphid
prayed for the mantis

watered   thinned lettuce
planted garlic and chives in the lettuce

radishes in the cucumber hills
marigolds among potatoes

studied all day the natural balance
of growth and injury

Now I cannot sleep

In the sky I watch
the procession
Each woman carries
a yellow bowl
Each walks in a line
on the sun's rim
The road is
black stone
their footprints
fossils
I hear sighs
in the bowls

The bowls are heads

I see myself
walk to the garden
black after rain
Vines run
in corridors
Cabbages are praying
their leaves
folding over
and over
Under a stone
I discover a fist
in the shape of a head
I plant it
It grows into a spire
a spire in the body
of a woman
her feet drawn
upward
her arms weighted
with fruit
the intimate
cracks of her body
flooded
with poppies

Now I cannot sleep

I let myself out
The garden is cold
I kneel
to the spire
risen out of the skull
Her throat moves
a river
in summer

"Tell me what you understand"
"I don't understand"

"Tell me why you did that"
"I don't know"

"Tell me what you were once"
"I am bleeding"

"Tell me what you are"
"I am blood"

THE SUN IN LOVE
WITH ITSELF

Weeks without rain   weeks
in a dry hex

Only the moon thrives
The air tightens

Voices prophesy
danse macabre

Mirages tremble

What I take for water
is distance

the blue sun of sandstorms

The only water here is sweat
and a wonder in the eye

of the waterbearer who must
be believing in pools

on whose skim of light
long-legged

green–billed birds reflect
and drink

Waiting for rain
I make stories

I am an old Chaldean

dreaming from a ziggurat
seams between stars

blueprints of ourselves
receding into distance

My grandfather traces
broken charts

Galaxies spin outward
like a fling of seed

In the last story I am blind
unacquainted with distance

I make a garden and love

lying down in the rain
and clay

making shapes
to take   to eat

FEASTING

In a large skillet heat oil
add onion garlic   green pepper
When the onion is transparent
remove to a bowl   reserve
Add zucchini eggplant
Mix gently   Add onion
tomatoes   Sprinkle
with parsley basil
Season   Uncover
and cook   Serve hot
or cold to friends
Tell stories

In the ancient story
the woman Lotah
buries her lover's
head in an earthen jug
After two hundred years
she unearths it
brews it with herbs
anoints her skin
and drinks

Thereafter
music falls in the rain
rain falls in her dreams
from which she rises
shaking out seeds
from her fingers
the smell of sperm
on her skin
She is granted
the power to die
over and over

Revising this plot
follow the lines
of my face
with your hands
When we touch
we honor the dead
who have raised us
When we harvest
and eat
we are whole

The garden grows into our bones

A SIMPLE ELEGY

I sew an Egyptian button
to a braid of black felt,
cord it about my neck.

Now I can talk about death.

An eight-petaled blossom
carved on bone
protects me.

If the flower
roots
let its speech

transplanted

be love.
For I must speak
of death in this house.

I like to think we grow
our own bodies
that we choose our parents
not always wisely
but according to need.
I needed pain
and silence
as much as love.
I was richly
rooted.

The deaths in this house
make me think of gifts:

how many hours, afternoons
how many closed doors
I was given
as the big people brooded
out loud or cursed silently—
I planted acorns
pinned a riverfall of red leaves
to the curtains, stared at the stars
pasted to the ceiling over my bed
giving them the names
I would call my children
touching my body
its small knobby fronds
with pleasure
and with sleep.

God was a terror
the Godfearing family
put in my closet
at night,
a wind that rasped
out of nowhere
rattling
the coathangers.

I suppose they confused
God with Death.

Deliberately
in the morning
I confused my father
reading prayers
over the scrambled eggs
and buttered toast
with God

and my mother with God
when she baked bread

and sang alto into the oven
to make the loaf
brown and rise.

In the bedroom closet
God shook his skin
and bones.

At Christmas dinner the family
joined hands around
the heavy table
blessing it and numbering
all who were not there,
Amma who loved mince pie
Dennis who would have wanted
the wing, grandfather
who spoke the loveliest
prayer on the violin.
The preacher said
they were all with us
in spirit. All flesh
is grass, he said, and I heard
glass, seeing all of us
suddenly in the lamplight
transparent figures
who could never hide anything.
We were all crystal and shining
and as the rest sang a hymn
of union for the living and dead
I wet my finger and ran it
around my lips until they rang
as clean as the tone of crystal,
Amen.

Years passed, marriages
rivalries. Gradually

my mother turned
the cupboard into lists
for her will.
She packed up glass
to save it.

My father grayed,
his mouth thinned
and turned down
as his mother's had.
A mole appeared
on the same plane
of his face as hers
and darkened.

I saw that the living
and dead sang hymns
together
but none of us
living together
sang.

Back for visits
I sat in the kitchen
with my mother at breakfast.
We broke silence
broke words.
We couldn't look
at each other simply

and say, *What matters*
is right now, this hot
coffee, the oranges,
the cat rubbing
the leg of the table.
Don't be afraid.

I learned the deaths
of three distant relatives
long-distance.

Don't come home, my mother
said. *There is nothing
really to be done.*

There is.

I work the garden
bake bread
to give to friends

tell the man I love
I want to have children
make words, close distances

be able to say
finally,
Undo this button.

Glass has been broken.
Floors must be swept clean,
flowers rooted

in jars of clear water
windows polished
opened out.

SIGNS: A PROGRESS
OF THE SOUL

White petals from the apple trees
have unhinged, blown
into my hair. A high wind
riffles the river,
and I write letters to everyone
fold messages in bottles
steal into marinas to scrawl
bold words on sails. Words
want to take wind.

I tell everyone, Listen
the world is a mirror
in which I see myself
coming toward
myself, never quite
closing the distance.
The one coming
to meet me has skin
like a mirror.
Often I cannot look
as the sun peaks
toward solstice.

I am restless
moved to dance
the two of us
risen in wind
just above the level
green wheat. I turn
slowly in pavane
slowly in love
court this one
I'll never meet
except in dance
but have always

lived with
as breath

After hours of picking peaches—
sunstruck—
I lie down in the grass,
don't know where I am.
Asleep in the sun, I wake
as I have for years
to a sense of light
to light
to light in the leaves
of these peach trees.

A child, I waked
once to a fire tree,
a flicker dreaming out.
I crawled into myself
to find it, vanished.
Older, I walked
on the sun, a dark-skinned
visionary attended by lions.
I saw this earth, spinning
in outer black space, turned
into paradise thickly planted
with lilies. I wanted
to get back.

From sleeping in the sun,
I wake to an earth hearth-hot.
I drowse, believing
sun is inside the earth
its center, the fire
orchard roots reach down to,
light which attaches us
to the earth, to the peach
to the flame-shaped seed
inside the peach.

When friends come, we agree
to work hard, make these stories,
our lives, just as we live them.

I want everything cleaned
up, linear.
I empty my mind
to blank paper,
rule it
straight—so.
Eat nothing
for days
but brown rice,
water. Keep
body fasted
pulled in thin
as bone.
Wipe tables
floors,
stack papers
screw lids on tight
throw out worn clothes
harvest, rake
put up the tomatoes
send letters, ask
What can I do
how serve
make amends?
I line up sins
examine
their labels
give up my attachment
to pleasure, ambition.
I want to be used
be practical
as this button
essential as salt.
Whoever's coming

I can wait.
I know what it means
to wait, to cut
through these hot
thick days
as the mower out
in the field
cuts hay
in a slow
analytical
sweep.

The sycamore blows,
yellow wind.
Wind drops.
Six o'clock
hush fills the river.
Last light
fills the bowl
of gold apples
and pears
on the kitchen table.
We are dancing.
Sun is crossing
the celestial equator
north to south.
It is falling.
Birds gather south.

Southing, autumnal
I follow the sun's arc
fall in love with you
dancing. You fall.
A wildhoney moon is rising,
evening tipping with weight
like a scale. Dancing
you are King David
joyfully coming home

dizzy with rhythm, falling
and rising with this wind
that shakes us, shakes apples
down, seeds
to the earth.

Today we tracked
wild bees to their hive
in the hollowing
windyellow wood,
brought home honey,
fruit of the falling
sun, elixir of pollen
and dance.
It will warm us
warm this kitchen
our dancing
through winter.

Cold. An unreasonable mist.
After supper I drink on the sly,
bourbon on the porch. Nobody's
here. I can just make out
the osprey's nest on the piling.
I'm not afraid of the dark.
I want you. Why aren't
you here? The osprey, mist
in its eyes, dives into the river,
renews its vision. So legend
says. And the phoenix
spices its nest, burns, dies
returns as a slender worm,
grows wings again, rises
again into the oarage of wings.
I think I'm a witch.
I died today three times
quickly, bright explosions
like sex, came back wanting

you to touch me all over
at once, river of you around me.
Will we ever be raised
incorruptible? I want
to be able to see to wherever
you are, look into myself, know
all the arguments by heart.
What am I hiding? Where
did I put it, the seed
the word that will sting me
back?

Dark, dark, dark.
There's always that blind
spot in the eye, part of the field
I look at, examine, can't see.
We must therefore keep
moving. Orion's my mentor.
The old ones who wanted me
to stay put forgot
to teach me not to believe
in revelation.
I put on a belt of hot coals,
stride through the dark.

Actually, we are together
reading the same book
in front of the fire.
We look thoroughly domestic.
There's a frost outside.
I'm tired from carrying wood.
Your hand's on my breast. Anyone
looking in should remember
the blind spot:
we're explorers.

I feel like the traveler
in the medieval woodcut
down on his hands and knees

on the earth, head
and shoulders clear through
an open seam he's found
in the cosmos.
I feel clear,
remember the blind spot
keep moving.

Under a crust of snow on the field,
below the frost line, I think seeds
radiate like fireflies in thick August.
We're making bread
for Christmas,

speak of marriage as bread, our tenderness
as the only bond between elements
worth having. Water yeast honey
flour salt—
we watch the sponge

then heavy dough rise. Punch down.
Light promises fullness.
In love with this process,
kneading I use my hands carefully.
We shape loaves, brush them with eggwash.

As they bake, we walk the field
to the river. It's glacial,
midnight. I'm barely breathing.
Who knows what will happen?
Dark presses over the field

until it's hard not to remember
fossils, the earth, this pause
between upheavals.
The river freezes white. We walk
back carefully, feeling the height

of mountains curve in the pulse . . .
in the field, hidden energies . . .

Unable to sleep, I wander
through the house. Three o'clock.
Outside, wind speckles with snow,
each flake an original word,
a world. In this room
amid rare books, an old pottery bowl
holds white African violets.
I water asparagus fern, speckled
angel wing, ivy.
I don't know what country
I've grown from. I am wind.

Where do we go from here?
asks the voice of the prophet.
Continents drift.
Faces of the dead
and the yet unborn
drift in my head.
Love drifts into dream
too distant from touch.
Think of a world with
no prisons, no prisoners.
I remember one man
a maker of words
who said simply,
Start from where you are.
Spread out. Nourish.
Reach. Be wind.

IN JANUARY, ONE MORNING . . .

the change in light alerts you—you want
a simple belief.
Blowing long steady breaths for fire in the kindling
you follow the ricochet of light moving in winged
shadows, as over water, continually beyond itself—
you realize the shape of light is its own
radiance.

Walking out past winter sumac in quiet fields
you find wind spread wide
and light—
last evening only a seam you split into wood—
spills from hollow pods, from each crack
and rent of this credible world, so clean
it suffices.